When a
Congregation
Cares

When a Congregation Cares

A New Approach to Crisis Ministries

Abraham & Dorothy Schmitt

Foreword by Jan C. Walker

HERALD PRESS
Scottdale, Pennsylvania
Kitchener, Ontario
1984

Library of Congress Cataloging in Publication Data
Schmitt, Abraham.
    When a congregation cares.
    1. Peer counseling in the church.   2. Group ministry.
I. Schmitt, Dorothy, 1928-   II. Title.   III. Title:
Crisis ministries.
BV4409.S36   1984   253   84-19294
ISBN 0-8361-3380-3 (pbk.)

WHEN A CONGREGATION CARES
Copyright © 1984 by Herald Press, Scottdale, Pa. 15683
    Published simultaneously in Canada by Herald Press,
    Kitchener, Ont. N2G 4M5. All rights reserved.
Library of Congress Catalog Card Number: 84-19294
International Standard Book Number: 0-8361-3380-3
Printed in the United States of America
Design by Gwen Stamm

90 89 88 87 86 85 84 10 9 8 7 6 5 4 3 2 1

*To the Mennonite Church
and to our home congregation
who taught us to care.*

•••••••••••••••

*All our lives we have heard that to follow Christ
we must be present in the other's pain. We were
shown how to bring healing through relating to
human hurts in the name of Christ.*

*Creating a congregational team approach
seemed a natural response to meet the needs of
hurting persons in a more effective way.*

Contents

Foreword

What can or should a caring congregation do for members who are experiencing distress in their marriage, a divorce, or some other crisis situation?

From firsthand experience Abraham and Dorothy Schmitt have written a bold and visionary book which proposes an answer to this most difficult question. It is an answer which involves the entire congregation. A team of carefully selected lay persons (with the knowledge and support of the pastor) relates to the person or persons involved in the crisis.

The model for ministry proposed by the authors is within the reach of most congregations. It offers potent possibilities for enhancing the ministries entrusted to the whole people of God and it is theologically sound.

Many of the illustrations used in the book center on the issues of divorce and remarriage. Such crises are all too frequently encountered in our churches. Many members are uneasy with the manner in which their congregation relates to troubled marriages. Nevertheless, as the reader will discover, the model for ministry proposed can be used to care for persons facing many other crisis situations as well.

Why approach a person in crisis with a caring team?

The reasons for doing so are many. Can the pastor handle all those crying for help in the breadth and depth required? Is it wise routinely to refer troubled members to experts who are not members of the congregation or to non-Christians? How does the person in crisis find those in the congregation who can help and are willing to do so? Do individuals who offer help to another member know how to relate that person to the entire fellowship? Cannot a team of carefully selected and trained persons provide more profound healing resources than an individual?

The authors rightly point out that many congregations have clinically trained counselors or therapists as members who are willing to care for others if they are invited to do so. They also testify to their belief that the primary function of the church is to proclaim the message of salvation and to do so through all members of the body. Their proposed model for ministry, the caring team, certainly is a way of putting flesh on the biblical mandate to do the works of love. (See Ephesians 4:12.)

When the authors turn their attention to describing the way in which the caring team functions and relates to the entire congregation, it becomes clear that they are writing out of the context of their experience as members of the Mennonite Church. This stance becomes clear when they discuss how the caring team relates to congregational structures and how the team assists the congregation to deal with persons who are divorced or contemplating remarriage.

I find their discussion of these matters instructive and helpful. Their unique perspective does not diminish the value of their contributions for other communities of faith.

Some months ago I sat at breakfast with Abraham Schmitt as he shared with me the messages of this book. The more I heard, the more excited I became not only to read the manuscript, but also to share the published book with members of the congregation to which I had recently been called. Why do I welcome this book? It resonates well with my 28 years of serving as an ordained minister in the Lutheran Church in America. For the past 14 years my work as an assistant to the bishop of a large Lutheran synod involved me in many crisis situations which I approached as a member of a caring team. On some occasions one of the team members was Abraham Schmitt. On no occasion did I fail to see the added healing power of a caring team!

What the Schmitts are proposing works also in settings other than a congregation. I have been involved in a caring team approach to ministry in the seminary milieu (where I served as an adjunct faculty member) as well as in the parish. I now serve as senior pastor in a parish of more than 1,200 members. I strongly endorse the use of caring teams for both theological and practical reasons.

During our breakfast conversation, Abe said he approached his work on the caring team from a clinical perspective. He wondered whether I was comfortable with such an approach in light of my experience as a pastor. I am.

In my opinion this book makes a clear and potent case for the caring team model of ministry. I delight in the way the book acknowledges God's call to exercise ministry in the Lord's name and then suggests a way of doing this.

I see this as a bold and visionary book because it requires a congregation and members of the caring team to tackle difficult life crises for which there are apparently no clear solutions. Risks must be taken if people are to become involved with each other in the depth of their lives.

It takes boldness for persons to work out contracts with each other and develop bonds of trust as they seek answers to difficult problems together. The kind of ministry proposed involves us at the center, not the periphery of life.

It takes vision to attempt to live out the proclamation of Ephesians 2:10: "God has made us what we are, and in our union with Christ Jesus he has created us for a life of good deeds, which he has already prepared for us to do" (TEV). It puts flesh on this call to ministry and does it for Jesus' sake.

The gospel, Paul tells us, is a gospel of friendship. "All this is done by God, who through Christ changed us from enemies into his friends and gave us the task of making others his friends also" (2 Corinthians 5:18, TEV).

When a Congregation Cares is a call to friendship. It is a way of dealing with the brokenness we all suffer as sinners and as members of a sinful race. It is a call for lay ministers to find effective ways to be stewards of their lives so that others may find a higher level of wholeness.

The church is not simply an institution, a denomination, or some other human contrivance. It is made up of people whom the Lord has linked to himself and to one another with bonds of love. To attempt to develop a model for being the church as we reach out to our sisters and brothers in the faith is profoundly theological and a task which is not reserved for those of us who are ordained.

Abraham and Dorothy Schmitt were baptized and called to be servants in Christ's church. This book is an expression of their ministry and a call to others to join them in reaching out to troubled persons for whom Christ also died. It is a challenging and tested plan for which I am profoundly grateful.

—Jan C. Walker, Pastor
Evangelical Lutheran Church
of the Holy Trinity, Akron, Ohio
(A congregation of the
Lutheran Church in America)

Authors' Preface

It is not possible to care unless one is willing to enter into another's pain. Congregations are already doing this. They take the words and example of Christ seriously as they feed the hungry, visit the sick, touch the lonely, and share the pain of congregational members or neighbors. Nevertheless, for an ever increasing group of persons the conventional response within the congregation is not sufficient.

Can congregations justifiably be asked to care more than they already do? We believe that this can be expected and also that an additional new form of caring should be considered by congregations. We propose that another form of caring is needed to respond effectively to persons who are experiencing mental illness, death in the family, marital disruption, divorce, remarriage, and other acute crises.

This book (1) describes a new model for caring; (2) reports on the effectiveness of the model after limited experimentation; and (3) shows how this model fits into the existing congregational structure. The book also describes how to begin the process, and sensitively develop a plan that fits into the uniqueness of the congregation and utilizes the gifts of its members.

The main distinction of this model is the use of a team approach to crisis intervention. We are borrowing a method used in crisis clinics and adapting it to congregational life. In these clinics a team evaluates each request for help. Persons representing psychiatry, psychology, social work, nursing, occupational therapy, and the like, do a full evaluation, using the unique professional orientation of each discipline to arrive at the most effective immediate response. The main motive for using the team approach is to intervene in a crisis as quickly and effectively as possible so that no more harm will be done.

The primary question addressed in this book is: Can a congregation use a team approach to care for and minister to persons in crisis? We believe that an appropriate modification of this clinic method can be transposed to a congregational setting.

The congregational team is composed of representatives from within the congregation. Members bring the distinctive gifts which they possess. A variety of caring roles are represented on the team—the pastor, an elder, a clinically trained person, and other congregational representatives. The team responds as members of a compassionate community. (At times they must speak out of their unique roles—the pastor from the pastoral role, the clinically trained person from that role). The team's mixed composition adds to its effectiveness.

A significant factor that should always be considered is that the central task of a caring team is to care for people. At times, the team must take a stand on moral, congregational, or spiritual issues. This is to be expected because the faith and practice of the congregation are involved. Although we accept that such stands must be taken, this must be done with the utmost compassion. A caring team should never participate in further hurting of persons. A tender touch must be used in all that is done.

An unfortunate aspect of this book is that so many of the illustrations deal with divorce and remarriage, and so few with the multitude of other crises that occur in the individual and group life of a congregation. This is true because we—the authors— have dealt personally with more of these situations and less of the other types.

Initially, the team of which we were a part came into existence as a result of our congregation's uneasiness in dealing with the divorce and remarriage issue. For the first number of years, the team was involved in only that area. Later, as other needs came to the attention of the team, additional crisis situations were included. Only recently has the team been assigned to a broader spectrum of troubled personal and interpersonal situations. It is our hope that as other congregations adopt this model, they will immediately open their doors to all acute needs.

To some, it might appear that a soft approach is used in dealing with the ethical issue of divorce and remarriage. This is a false impression. The congregation and team members represented in this book stand firm on the biblical injunction that God's ultimate will is that marriage should be permanent as stated in the marriage vows. Anything less than that is sin. Because a team is willing to struggle with each person caught in sin does not mean that sin is condoned. In order to stay deeply involved and enter into the pain and agony of the sinner, the team chose to be redemptive in responding to crises because this offered opportunity for caring and redemption to those in crises.

Another reason for imbalance in the team involvement in divorce and remarriage might be that a congregation that dares to open itself to crisis ministry may well find that marital breakups comprise the first major influx of critical situations. This is due to the fragile state of marriages today.

There is a price to pay for beginning this type of ministry. Because we believe in the forgiveness of sin, in redemption through Christ, and in the spiritual wholeness that the church proclaims, our congregation chose to respond whenever and in whatever way it could.

As this team approach is utilized by other congregations, our hope is that the entire scope of needs will be included. Perhaps the model for caring will take a totally different form.

What is the best name for this team?

One congregation called it the crisis ministry team. The task of the team is to respond, by intervention or referral, to acute crises in the lives of its members. No crisis is considered too severe to respond to in some way. But the title *crisis ministry* leaves the impression that the team responds only in extreme events. This should not be the case.

We chose the term *caring team* for use in this book, to make the team's responsibility more general. Whenever there is a call for help, the team should respond. However, this may leave the faulty impression that a team does the essential caring in a congregation. Every member of a congregation needs to care, and keep on caring, even though a team approach is adopted. Also, team caring is not a higher form of caring. It is simply a specialized, more concentrated form. Hopefully, each congregation can come up with a name for its caring group that is most appropriate to the role of the team in that particular congregation.

Chapter 10 illustrates how one congregation adopted this model. They called it the *caring core*—meaning that the team is the core of caring in that congregation. This is how they preferred to symbolize it.

Another congregation called it the *counseling ministry team*. (The guidelines for this team are included in appendix A.) The focus here is on the fact that the uniqueness of the team is that it offers counseling. The value of this title is that it does not imply that the team replaces other caring or is a higher form of caring than already occurs in the congregation.

One valid criticism is that the model shared in this book is presented too positively. The illustrations emphasize success rather than failure.

We do not apologize for the fact that we are extremely excited about our participation in helping develop a congregational team approach to caring. Our enthusiasm may have slanted our ability always to perceive accurately. However, optimism has a way of being contagious and may help others catch the zeal for reconciliation and restoration.

It was remarkable how the group members freely gave themselves to most persons who asked for the team's help for as long as was needed. In response, they sought wholeness. With that degree of momentum pushing for spiritual health, how could there not be positive results? At times it seemed like God, in a special way, heard our pleas. With the continuing prayer support of the congregation, God broke through in wonderful ways.

We acknowledge that the initial experiment grew out of a unique congregational setting. Caring for persons has been an important part of the life of this congregation throughout its long history. When the caring team emerged it was not a startling event. Simultaneously, class shepherds were selected to look out for the welfare of small groups of members and to mobilize others to respond to explicit needs. A board of elders was always vigilant in ministering to members. Other persons were set aside for the task of deaconing the elderly, the sick, and the needy. This fertile setting aided the first caring team. However, that does not mean that all of these conditions must be present to begin a caring team.

The more a congregation is oriented toward being a community of believers, and the more ready a congregation is to create new models for caring, the easier it will be for a caring team to begin and to thrive. God planted the seeds of compassion long before this model was proposed, but there could hardly have been a more appropriate soil for that seed to grow.

Briefly, then, this book is an effort to demonstrate that a team approach to caring is feasible within a congregation. We shall also attempt to define clearly the way a congregation can go about setting up and training a caring team. Many case illustrations will be used to demonstrate how the team may interact in a healing process.

The case material in this book is drawn from a number of congregations with whom we were involved in the creation of caring teams. At times, composite illustrations are used to disguise the identity. This means that a variety of sources were used to compose a single episode. In all cases the material is so disguised that it would not be recognizable by the individuals or congregations involved.

We wish to express gratitude to our home congregation for their wisdom in seeing the need for a caring team. Their willingness to experiment with this model allowed us to use our gifts in a creative way as the model evolved.

To the several other congregations who accepted our model and us as we helped them begin, we are grateful.

We also wish to acknowledge our gratitude to the pastors who adapted their style of ministry to enable a caring team to function.

In addition, we are indebted for the case material which was used from all of these experiences. To further disguise the illustrations used in the text, the various sources are not named.

We especially wish to acknowledge several readers: Paul M. Lederach, John R. Martin, Paul M. Zehr, and Harold Bauman, who personally demonstrated the meaning of the caring ministry as they exercised a labor of love in offering many helpful suggestions for changes in the manuscript.

—Abraham and Dorothy Schmitt
Souderton, Pennsylvania

When a
Congregation
Cares

1

A Family in Financial Crisis

A rt and Mary have been a part of the congregation for many years. It is general knowledge that they have trouble managing their money. Mismanagement is the first idea that strikes people when another item of news about them is circulated.

Jim, a senior executive officer of the bank, also a member of this congregation, knew the real financial story of this couple. He had dealt with them in many of their crises. His bank had provided the mortgage on the family farm plus a number of other loans. He had helped them refinance their indebtedness on a number of occasions. The failure of this couple to meet their mortgage payments was due to come up at a bank board meeting. Jim knew that the majority of the board would vote for foreclosure of Art's and Mary's mortgage and to take possession of their real estate and their large herd of beef animals.

Jim was deeply distressed over the events that he saw transpiring. He knew that the action was appropriate from the bank's perspective. Actually, the bank had gone overboard for Art and Mary and it was time to call a halt to it. Logically, as a banker, he should vote in favor of foreclosure. In his heart, as a member of the congregation, he protested violently. Should one not forgive seventy times seven as Jesus said? Where is love in a predicament like this?

At the bank's inevitable board meeting Jim requested that no action be taken until he could find out exactly what was wrong in that household. Without a specific course of action in mind, he was able to convince the board to table the issue for one month.

Mentally, he wondered what his congregation could do. A request would be especially difficult since he had pleaded on their behalf on other occasions. A number of years earlier he had rallied a Sunday school class to make a special donation. Also, most of the congregation remembered the time the church had paid $7000 on an overdue mortgage for Art and Mary. Jim did not feel he should approach the church for this kind of bailout again.

The story of Art and Mary was well known. Mary was the daughter of a hard-working family. Her father had even been an administrator of a church-related retirement center. Since the father was not properly certified for the position, he had to step down to a lower position and was replaced by a younger man who was also a member of this same congregation. Their living style was quiet, unassuming, and modest. Mary was shy and felt inferior. She had been diligent in the care of her own five children, now in their early teens through young adulthood. The many humiliations of her life appeared to have taken a toll on her. Even her stooped posture seemed to conform to her image of an inadequate person on the verge of despair.

Art had always been an unpredictable type of person. He was an only child of elderly parents who had died a number of years ago. As far as anyone could remember, they had always lived in the hired hand's house on a modest farm where his father had always worked. Even as a child Art was part of the farm life, though nothing of his personality fitted life on the farm. He was an artistic type of person who spent many hours painting and playing a variety of musical instruments. He had a host of grandiose ideas of what he would do, someday, with his many talents. He never settled on any one form of art, but dabbled in many. Much of his time was spent in fantasizing about lofty artistic possibilities.

In college, Art tested a series of majors, some in art and some in musical fields. It was obvious that he was not outstanding in any of them. After dropping out of college, he returned to work on the same farm as his father. Then he enrolled in a local agricultural college, with the assumption that he could succeed there. He obtained a master's degree and then accepted a low-level teaching position in the agricultural college. Although he continued dutifully to carry out his tasks until the present time, he simply did not fit the assignment. At heart, he felt that he was still to be a noteworthy artist or musician. During these years he married Mary and a number of children were born in what seemed quick order for both of them.

When the farm became available, he wanted it desperately. With the help of the elderly owner who held a large mortgage, and the bank, he made the deal. Now he could prove his expertise in raising a herd of beef cattle. Fortunately, he did not give up his teaching position.

The general impression Art left was that he was a misplaced artist who accidentally was farming and teaching. His lack of common sense and his heightened idealism proved to be costly rather than profitable.

On a number of occasions individuals, as well as Sunday school classes and other groups, had come to his rescue. At one time a group project was organized to repair all of his fences, because Mary had to herd the cattle while she should have been taking care of the children and he had to be at the college. Art could not seem to get organized to take care of the problem himself.

In the congregation, there was a general sense that this whole farm family setup was heading for disintegration, though they did not realize how rapidly this was occurring.

After the bank board meeting, Jim called Art and Mary and asked if the pastor might join them for a serious discussion on finances. Jim had to underscore to Art that he was the subject of an earlier bank board meeting for him to accept that this meeting was necessary.

The four met at Art and Mary's farmhouse during the day while all the children were away. A walking tour of the farm permitted Art to expound on his many farfetched plans. Jim responded with, "Art, you are a dreamer! The bank will no longer accept your dreams as notes."

When they moved indoors, Mary tearfully told her story. She confided that she was exhausted having to do the farm work that Art left undone. Art objected by declaring that her problem was that she refused to make the children do the work after they became teenagers or young adults. Then Mary unburdened her feelings. She said that the children refused to do anything because they hated the farm. They knew it had been the subject of endless grief. It was their dad's unrealistic dream and they wanted no part of it. Mary mentioned that a number of creditors had been calling the house, and a large number of credit card companies had refused them additional credit and were demanding payment on overdue installment bills.

The pastor listened sensitively as he reflected on the options for responding to them. He wondered if this entire situation might benefit from a congregational caring team. At first he thought that a separate group of informed persons might be called upon. He dismissed this idea because he knew those persons were also available for the existing team to call. Before leaving the farm the pastor called the chairman of the team to check out the appropriateness as well as the best immediate response. They agreed to arrange a meeting of the team as soon as possible and to see if Jim, and Art and Mary could all be there for the first session.

Jim's presence, representing the bank, would be helpful to define the severity of the problem, which Art tended to underestimate. The chairman also knew about Art's grandiose dreams and that facing reality as soon as possible was essential.

At first Art objected to having their problem become the subject of a congregational group. "Maybe there could be another Sunday school class offering. This would bail me out now. Then when my animals are ready for sale, I'll be all right again."

Jim quickly reminded Art that he was much too deeply in debt to be bailed out so easily. Besides, Art was also faced with the fact that it was known within the congregation and the community that when he sold a herd of cattle a few years ago he had invested it in a risky get-rich-quick scheme and had lost the money.

"Granted the members of the congregation have been very generous," Jim said. "But will they respond the same way now that they know about your investment error? You had better take the route suggested by the pastor." Art then accepted that the meeting was necessary.

The team, which included the pastor, met with Art and Mary and Jim on a suitable evening in the church library. This was a tearful and painful session of further disclosure. The climax came when Mary exclaimed that she was tired of covering up for Art and that she could not take one more call from a creditor. If there was no relief in sight, she said that she was going to bail out of the marriage. She also said that as far as her nerves were concerned, this session had come none too soon.

Since the first action that needed to be taken was to find a way to deal with finances and debts, all efforts were turned to this. Suddenly Jim came up with a proposal. He said that he would volunteer to work with Art and Mary, if they promised to continue to meet with the caring team and to cooperate with him until the end. The terms he suggested were (1) he wanted to meet with them at their home to review their entire financial picture, (2) all credit cards must be destroyed, and (3) that no more debts could be incurred without his approval. He also said that it might mean that he would take over all financial management for them, including the cashing of Art's paycheck. If Art trusted their true intentions, then Jim would approach the bank board to have them put the mortgage and other loan payments on hold. Jim arranged for his meeting with Art and Mary, and the team also scheduled a session with them.

In the second session with the caring team, Art and Mary each talked. The team members were touched by Art's story. His aspirations had been so high, and yet failure had been his lot, rather than success. Someone noted that an only child often has a difficult time separating dreams from reality because there are no siblings to help. Then Art said that he felt as though he had brothers and sisters gathered around him now for the first time in his life and that it felt good since these were his real brothers and sisters in Christ.

This celebration ended abruptly when someone turned to Mary. She said that she had talked with the children about the financial crisis and told them that they were in the process of settling it with a group from the church. The children's unanimous plea was "Mom, tell Dad to get rid of the cows."

Art was visibly shaken by this declaration. He knew that he had expected them to help and had called them lazy and spoiled. After all, this was no more than his own dad had expected from him. An extensive sorting process occurred and Art requested time to talk with Mary and the children about the matter one more time.

Meanwhile Jim worked systematically with the couple on finances. He notified the chairman of the team that Art and Mary and he had reached a consensus. A meeting was arranged to report to the team.

The moment the couple and the team met with Jim it was obvious that the news was bad. The entire farming operation had, in fact, been a financial loss and other earnings had been used to keep the farm afloat. All of the livestock needed to be sold immediately. Jim reported that the bank board objected to his proposal, but accepted it on the condition that all of Art's loans be refinanced and that a major sum of money had to be paid soon. This made the sale of the livestock mandatory.

The bank board also agreed that Jim should assume full responsibility for all financial matters for the couple. Jim discovered that both Art and Mary engaged in impulse buying which, considering their financial status, was inappropriate. When they began talking about buying habits, both admitted they were involved. Art said that he always had difficulty with his urge to buy. He said that he never really had been taught how to use money. His parents always had given him what he wanted even when they should not have. Mary said that impulse buying was not her normal pattern, but that she was so frustrated by the bondage in the other parts of her life that she often spent money in vengeance. The team agreed that some new form of handling the money was necessary.

It was several months before the team met again. There was so much that had to be done by Jim and Mary and Art that it seemed that the team's agenda with them could wait.

By the next meeting, most of the financial rearrangements were completed. The livestock was gone. The children and Mary were greatly relieved. Art was grieving, but he was willing to talk about it and then go on with life.

During the next several sessions when the team met with Art and Mary, their discussion centered around Mary learning money management from Jim and from a class she was attending. The team helped Art own up to the fact that money management was not his area and that he should accept Mary taking over their finances, even though he did not like it. Art also needed help to see that this did not undermine his masculine role. He talked at great length about his need to feel like a real man. As an only child, he could not work this out with any brothers and sisters. His father had been a decidedly weak role model. His mother was artistic and he was like her in that respect. However, he had attempted to succeed in his father's vocation and failed. To admit now that he really was unable to handle money was a blow.

The team continues to meet with this couple. The handling of money remains an issue. Mary feels a lot better about their money situation. The children are greatly relieved because they wanted to participate with their peers without the constant farm work hanging over their heads. Art is asking the team to stick by him until he finds a more meaningful role in life.

Should a congregation make this entire process its business? We are emphatically saying, "Yes, it should." Caring is the very nature of love for one's brothers and sisters in the congregation. This is a very diverse task — one to which many congregations cannot respond as they now function.

2

A Team Approach to Caring

Several years ago Hilda had an emotional breakdown. After her hospitalization she found it difficult to return to church services. Hilda was aware that most people knew about her hospital experience because it was announced publicly and an explanation had been given to many people. Also, the effects of the illness on her appearance could not be hidden. So it was a struggle to meet people again. She had stopped by the pastor's office on several occasions and he encouraged her to continue trying to get involved.

After a while, it was easier to appear in public, but Hilda still felt ill at ease wondering how much each person knew whenever anyone talked with her. She carefully worded her phrases with the hope that people would consider her fully recovered. The struggle continued within Hilda, and she thought she had no one to talk to about this dilemma. Her therapist and the pastor were helpful, but she needed other persons to relate to her comfortably.

Hilda listened carefully when a new style of caring was introduced in her congregation. She had felt that people in her congregation had been kind and reached out to her. However, because of the acute crisis she had experienced, she needed extra care. She hoped this new style of caring would meet her need.

Soon after the team began functioning, Hilda asked the pastor if the team was meant for her. He invited her to meet with them at the next meeting.

During the next several sessions with the caring team, Hilda was encouraged to retell her story. The team asked her about her past and how she understood what had happened to cause the breakdown, to tell about her hospital experience, as well as to share her feelings toward her current therapy process. She felt relieved that, at last, a group of concerned people from her own congregation could hear her story and would understand her struggle with mental illness.

There was no need for many formal meetings with the team. Hilda was told that they would be available at any time when she cared to talk, informally at church events, by telephone, or that she could ask to meet with the team again.

After her meetings with the team, Hilda felt different about returning to services. When the old fear came back on Sunday morning she reflected on the team or on individual members of the group. Hilda appreciated that several persons were available for her if she needed to talk. It almost felt as though the staff or her fellow patient friends from the hospital, who had come to mean so much to her, were with her at congregational events. Hilda now had a replacement for these friendships as part of her congregational life.

Hilda felt especially good when she noticed several team members looking for her at congregational meetings. When they noticed her, smiles were exchanged. It simply mattered that someone who knew her whole story cared that she was present. Hilda needed someone to care enough to want her to be there. It was good that she didn't have to reply to a team member with the usual, "Fine, thank you," as she always thought she had to when someone else asked her how she felt. She could now tell them that she had not slept well the night before and that it might be due to her change in medication. It was good not to have to pretend that all was well. The congregation had become a new therapeutic community which cared for her.

Even though she did not need to call a team member, at least she had been given an invitation. That felt precious.

The team responded simply, but correctly for Hilda, and that was what made the difference. "But," she reflected, "isn't that what the church ought to do for me?"

How can a congregation really care for hurting members like Hilda? How can a body of compassionate persons reach out effectively to those who are overcome by acute crises?

An unusual situation exists in many congregations. Most members of the average congregation are caring persons in times of crises. They demonstrate this by sharing human love, as well as by sharing God's love which they experience through Christ. However, many persons suffer from frustration and guilt for not responding to the deeper ongoing needs around them. The biggest problem is that they do not know how to respond, nor is there a systematic way for responding built into the congregation's program.

Members receive a clear message that they are to carry one another's burdens. They are to love one another. They hear this from the pulpit and know this is the basic position of the church and an underlying theme of the gospel.

Yet, in this very setting, interacting with fellow church members and listening to this same profound proclamation, there are persons who are silently crumbling. There are individuals who are overcome by personal, financial, relational, or marital and family problems. Some are living with infidelity or alcoholism. Others are lonely, maladjusted, or interpersonally crippled and may be slipping into discouragement, despair, depression, or even mental illness. The list could go on.

The people who can help are nearby, but the ones who need help really can't reach them. Hurting persons often leave the church service as frustrated as when they arrived. There is no organized way to bring together those who are willing to help and those who need help.

Experiencing this in our own congregation, a gnawing message became louder and clearer to us. "Why doesn't someone take a hold of this situation?" Then the message finally changed to, "Why don't *we* take a hold of this problem?" When we did, an unusual series of events occurred.

This is the story of what happened as we shared our experience with several other congregations and the story of how a unique model for helping emerged. It is possible to utilize the unique gifts of congregational members in a systematic and organized way, to respond to persons who are hurting, who are overwhelmed, or who are falling apart. The overflowing compassion of some persons can help heal the unbearable wounds of others. This is a model to aid congregations in developing a caring response to deeply hurting and troubling situations.

In all congregations there are resourceful people who do respond to persons in need. Most pastors spend many hours dealing with one crisis after another. Many pastors are also becoming skillful in counseling. So it is not uncommon for pastors to have needy persons from the congregation and the community passing through their offices. Often, members of boards of elders, or deacons, also reach out to needy persons who come to their attention. Many meeting hours are spent wrestling with a particularly troublesome situation which requires a response.

Many congregational members are also sensitive to the friendless, ailing, and destitute individuals who need someone near. They respond as they can in time of need.

In recent years more clinically trained therapists and counselors, who are members of congregations, make themselves available as they are asked to assist. Special classes on parenting or on marriage relationships are taught by them. These persons also may be asked to contribute major input to the congregation on interpersonal dynamics. However, as a whole, many of their clinical skills and gifts are not used. They go home from church knowing that they must wait until they arrive at their clinical offices before their gifts and training can be put to work. Although they know they have the skill to respond to the hurts in the congregation, there is no avenue to utilize their skills.

There are also many small groups that search for needy persons and take them into their folds. Some congregations have small groups whose task it is to edify each other and to offer sympathetic support for persons in their group. At other places, friendship groups have been created who also are alert for needy persons outside their group who can be helped.

When a concrete need emerges, many congregations rally around that particular need and organize with their full effort until it is alleviated.

All of this is excellent. However, the missing element is a central body of persons who have the skills and experience to respond to situations which need special help, and can synchronize these resources of the congregation on an ongoing, organized, and systematic basis.

Our congregation faced this issue ten years ago and began to wrestle with a complex dichotomy. In our congregation there was a large reservoir of caring and competent persons wanting to do good. Also, there were persons who desperately needed help. Yet there was no effective way for them to get together.

A caring group who used a team approach to respond to hurting persons or situations was formed. This team then became an arm of the congregation empowered to act for the total congregation when needed.

Both the congregation and the pastor no longer saw the pastor's office as the primary healing center of the congregation for all troubled situations. The pastor continued to see individuals as before, but he always knew that there was another resource that he could consider as an option for helping the persons he saw privately. The team also stood by the pastor to seek the most appropriate healing response. The elders no longer had to find an answer for each crisis situation they faced. They could refer it to a team of competent, committed persons who were ready to intervene in any situation. Members knew that, if in their attempt to do good they suddenly found a situation which overwhelmed them, they could lead individuals to a helping, healing group that was also part of their congregation. Hurting members of the congregation also knew that they had a confidential forum to turn to when they needed it.

A great change also occurred for clinically trained persons in this team approach. They now were asked to utilize the essence of their gifts, training, and skills in the service of the congregation. In this new capacity, a trained counselor can become a valuable aid in enabling the team to function. This does not mean that a counselor is more needed or valuable than any other team member. It only means that there is someone available who is already trained in utilizing a team approach to deal with people in crises. The trained counselor also has developed the skill of helping a group of persons exercise their gifts so that a healing process can occur. Trained counselors should be able to assess the needs of the hurting person, to facilitate the flow of events, and to suggest the intervention that must occur to utilize the team in such a way that healing can result. The most essential skill is to be able to rally a group of able persons to respond effectively by providing the bridge between the needs of the hurting individual or couple and the resources of the congregation.

There is value in having a clinically trained counselor on the team, but this may be unrealistic for many smaller or rural congregations. A smaller congregation might use a clinically trained person from outside the congregation to train one or more members of the team. There are many caring persons who can learn to keep confidences and respond in ways which bring healing to individuals.

Nevertheless, there are many clinically trained persons available and they may be eager to be used. Using the model described, congregations may be challenged to call appropriately upon individuals with these gifts. And these persons will have the chance to respond to an opportunity which has been presented to them. We also believe that many more persons will get the necessary training if they see that their talents can be used as an integral part of congregational life.

A caring team, focusing God's power within a congregation, can bring healing in an effective manner to those who stand in need of help. It is a method of putting into practice the gospel in the spirit and with the compassion of Christ.

The team proposed here responds to a call for help from a number of directions.

One type of call comes directly to the team from the hurting, ailing, or sinning person. Anyone in need of a healing ministry should feel free to ask for help, knowing that the team will respond.

Another type of call for help from the team comes from caring persons who see their brothers and sisters in Christ stumbling. Such a call may come from ordained leaders of the congregation, elders, shepherds, or from any of the members. The hurting individual or couple may be approached directly and pointed toward the team. Or the team may be approached and alerted to the needs of an individual or couple.

The team may decide to meet with persons who appear to need help. As the team surveys the congregation, they observe hurting and struggling persons. Team members may approach and invite such persons into the healing process. In some cases members who are losing out in the Christian life may need to be tapped on the shoulder and invited to meet with the team.

Referrals may also come from within the congregation. The congregation may establish policies which explicitly state under what conditions the team is requested to act on behalf of the body. When such situations arise the team would initiate a counseling process, and the members in need would be expected to respond and become involved. Membership in the congregation would include willingness to give and receive counsel.

A congregation may decide that every couple anticipating marriage should be asked to meet with the team as part of the premarital preparation. Anyone involved in infidelity, separation, divorce, or remarriage also may be expected to meet with the team for its healing ministry.

3

A Model for Healing

At a workshop conducted on caring and reconciliation, a participant gave the following illustration. The congregation was faced with a request for a wedding ceremony from a member who was planning marriage to a divorcé. In every area of life the couple believed and lived within the guidelines of the church, except for the crucial issue of the remarriage. They exemplified their commitment to the church by their willingness to submit to anything that the congregation requested of them. Although the divorcé was not a member, he too was willing to participate in whatever was asked of him, including joining the church, if they would grant permission for marriage.

This request resulted in the congregation beginning a study process of their position on divorce and remarriage. Because the congregation had not really faced up to the issue prior to this request, the study took many months. During this time the couple quietly slipped away to join another church where the question of divorce and remarriage was not a crucial issue.

The congregation finally ended their study approving the acceptance of divorced individuals if they demonstrated a biblical faith and sought forgiveness for sins committed. However, the couple who had initiated the study of the question had vanished long ago. Surely there must be another way.

To create a model for healing brokenness in the congregation, in all aspects of relationships and living, seemed too great an undertaking. However, the need was starkly evident, so it became a challenge our congregation accepted. These criteria were established: (1) the model must be workable and easily adopted by most congregations; (2) it must be biblical and fulfill Christ's mandate to the church; (3) it must utilize the gifts of persons within the congregation and not assign this task to others; and (4) it must bring both emotional and spiritual healing to individuals, and thus be both biblically and therapeutically sound.

In developing the model we incorporated a number of biblical teachings and principles.

The first is that the congregation is viewed as the priesthood of all believers. "But you are a chosen people, a royal priesthood, a holy nation, a people belonging to God, that you may declare the praises of him who called you out of darkness into his wonderful light" (1 Peter 2:9). In the Old Testament the priestly role in interceding between God and humanity was assigned to a special person. However, in the new era this mediating task belongs to all members of a congregation. In the royal priesthood role we carry out all our work, including the work of the caring team. With this sacred commission we minister to those in need, offering ourselves and them to God, and asking God to minister to all.

A second biblical principle is that the gifts of all members of a congregation are given to perform special tasks. This, too, is a clear position of the New Testament. "Now about spiritual gifts, brothers, I do not want you to be ignorant. . . . There are different kinds of gifts, but the same Spirit. There are different kinds of service, but the same Lord. There are different kinds of working, but the same God works all of them in all men. Now to each one the manifestation of the Spirit is given for the common good. To one there is given through the Spirit the message of wisdom, to another the message of knowledge by means of the same Spirit, to another faith by the same Spirit, to another gifts of healing by that one Spirit. . . . All these are the work of one and the same Spirit, and he gives them to each man, just as he determines" (1 Corinthians 12:1, 4-9, 11).

It is on the basis of this concept of the distribution of gifts that the caring team can function. Certain members can be asked by the entire body of believers to carry out a special task on behalf of the others. Also, as unique needs arise the team can call upon the gifts of other members of the congregation to minister in various areas.

There are several assumptions that we have used as guidelines.

In most situations, the problems of hurting individuals or marital relationships cannot be handled by the congregation as a whole. Attempts to include everyone often result in division and confusion. Too often individuals or couples involved will not remain long enough to await the outcome. Such a process may result in more harm than good.

Delicate issues such as brokenness in individual lives, or in marriage relationships among members, should not become a topic for open debate or intervention by a large group of persons. If a congregation wishes to have a conference to study its doctrinal position on a general issue, such as divorce and remarriage, the entire congregation should be involved, but the study process should not be initiated by the problems of a particular person or couple caught in the throes of crisis.

Leaving the decision up to the pastor alone is an inadequate solution. This may place a pastor in an impossible situation in which he will be criticized for whatever he does. The process of dealing with acute individual or marital problems, including troubled premarital counseling, couples in stress, separation, divorce, and remarriage, should not be dependent solely on the pastor. The congregation must claim ownership for the problems, as well as be involved in providing solutions. This does not mean that the pastor is not an integral part of the process. However, the problems are not his alone. The burdens can also be shared by the congregation.

There are two ways that a congregation can act responsibly in acute crises. The first is to study the issues as they emerge. Exactly where does the church stand in relation to the spirit of

Christ, the Scriptures, and the society in which it finds itself? There is a need to establish congregational policies. An additional way is to establish a caring team which will respond to every specific crisis situation in light of congregational policies. If the congregation has defined its position clearly, it is easier for the team to be able to speak for the congregation in each individual crisis.

In many congregations no group is prepared to assume ongoing responsibility for these problems. The board of elders or a spiritual life committee may be called upon to act when a particularly troublesome situation arises. This usually happens when the problem is scandalous and some action must be taken. Such boards or committees are capable of making recommendations on behalf of the congregation. They may request God's help through prayer. However, more steps and a lot of experience and skill are usually necessary in dealing with very troubled situations.

Here is an illustration of a case which caught everyone in a congregation off guard. The board of elders consulted us about an impossible predicament they had faced some time ago. It was too late for their current situation, but they hoped to be better prepared for their next problem.

A rather hasty marriage had occurred between two middle-aged persons, Hugo and Helen, whose first mates had both died. Hugo was a self-made, self-centered person who had succeeded in the business world. He expected to have his own way since vocationally, and in his first marriage, there were no questions asked. He felt no need to be accountable to anyone. At frequent intervals he dined out with Helen which she appreciated. She asked for little more from the marriage. He also attended church services regularly and was outgoing, gregarious, and equally generous with the congregation.

What Helen found completely intolerable was that Hugo often entertained so-called female clients in a most elaborate style. He claimed it was a routine part of his vocation. Helen suggested to him that something else was going on. Hugo simply denied it and continued living his own life, but now he stopped informing her where or with whom he was. He assumed that it was his private concern and not hers.

After approximately six years, this couple separated causing a major crisis in the congregation. Too many persons became involved. Both Hugo and Helen had many relatives in the congregation who tended to side with their kin. Officials of the congregation were frequently contacted with new information and the continued request that somebody had better do something since the whole situation was unbecoming to Christians and especially to members of this fellowship. The more the pastor and the board of elders attempted reconciliation, the more they found themselves caught in incriminating gossip and conflicting stories.

It was well known that Hugo's lifestyle made marriage to him difficult. There was a deceptive quality about him which was hard to define. Yet overtly he was a diligent church member.

Since Helen initiated the separation, people generally found it hard to square her actions with the "until death do us part" vow that she had taken before all of them.

Then for several years things quieted down. They lived in separate apartments. Hugo attended services, participated in all church events, and gave liberally. Helen found another church home. The uneasy truce bothered many people. Hugo's sexual fidelity was often questioned.

Finally, Helen filed for a divorce. It was immediately assumed that someone else had entered her life, and remarriage was planned. As soon as Hugo received the legal notice, he asked for a session with the board of elders. Since Hugo knew the congregation's position on divorce and remarriage, he could eloquently plead his case. He even challenged the elders to be the redemptive church and take appropriate action to bring Helen back to him. Hugo proclaimed loudly his beliefs, faith in the church, and the need for literal obedience to God's Word. He now expected the elders to counsel Helen. To add more prestige to his position Hugo freely informed fellow members of the congregation about his request for reconciliation and that it was Helen who would not yield.

The session the elders set up with Helen was a fiasco. In an effort to get to the truth of what really had gone wrong in the marriage, the meeting became an inquest. Since Helen felt her reputation was being pitted against Hugo's, she revealed more incriminating information about Hugo. She shared some plausible evidence that Hugo had been unfaithful to her in the marriage and, without question, had been involved with other women during the separation. When it came to suggesting what should be done, the elders disagreed. One elder felt compelled to cite Scripture on the sacredness of the marriage vows and the eternal penalty which would result from failure to live up to them. When challenged by Helen about whose was the greater sin, to have had extramarital sex or to have walked out on a marriage, the elder declared that to break a vow taken before God was worse, because that meant a person remained in a broken state before God. The other elders unsuccessfully tried to stop this futile interchange.

The final episode came when Helen wanted to know why the elders involved themselves at this time. They had known there was difficulty for years. They did not respond then. Why now? She had painfully begun putting her life together. Now that there was hope for the future, why did the elders cause this enormous eruption? She even asked whether the elders weren't really being goaded on by Hugo, and being used as pawns by him to make him appear holy in the eyes of the church. Emotionally, Helen could not handle reconciliation.

The meeting ended leaving new scars. Nothing had been solved. At this point the elders desperately needed a new approach and asked for help to face future situations.

This book suggests an alternative which meets the criteria mentioned at the beginning of this chapter: the creation of a caring team, empowered by the congregation, and equipped with the skills to take full responsibility for issues related to troubled persons and to troubled marriages in the congregation. This team acts on behalf of the congregation as a whole. The team's mandate is to act redemptively with each person, or couple, where there is hurt, sin, or error.

If this congregation had used a caring team approach, many things in the relationship of Hugo and Helen could have been different.

Hugo and Helen should have been helped to look at the reason for their haste in getting married. Persons in a hurry to get married often are trying to tie the knot before any disruptive truth can be revealed.

An evaluation of their personality traits and their lifestyles would have suggested potential conflict. If they still had desired to proceed with marriage, Helen at least would have known about Hugo's flamboyant habits, and Hugo would have realized that Helen was not infinitely tolerant. Several sessions with a caring team would have revealed these personality traits.

Later, either one of them could have called upon the caring team to help them face the crises long before separation became the only option. If there had been a forum to air their differences early, they might have negotiated a compromise.

In the eventuality of separation, the caring team would have taken action to keep the separation less destructive and would have sought to bring about healing.

Several strategies, carefully planned and guided, could have been used by a team to deal with Hugo and Helen.

From the beginning of the courtship, this couple could have been seen jointly by the caring team to learn to know them and help build a positive relationship for any future ministry with them. In this way the team would not have been caught in the middle of disparate stories. Each of them would have told their views of what had gone wrong in the presence of their mates.

Also, Hugo and Helen could have been asked not to elicit sympathy from persons within the congregation who would side with them during the disintegration of the marriage. They should have been invited to use the team alone to vent their hurts rather than to turn inappropriately to relatives and friends.

As a last resort, if all hope of reconciliation had been lost, the team could have helped them arrive at an amicable parting. This also would have avoided dividing the congregation into camps.

It was apparent that Hugo and Helen could not guide their relationship through the narrow harbor even under good conditions. Then when the storms broke, their vessel ran aground. At times like these, a skilled harbor pilot who has traveled this way many times is needed. The caring team could have served this function for Hugo and Helen.

To understand this model a diagram may be helpful. Figure 1 shows the circles of caring in a congregation. A large circle represents the entire congregation. This also suggests that whatever happens within this largest circle is the responsibility of every member. In the same way, responsibility for personal or marital failures and reconciliation belongs to everyone.

Figure 1
The Circles of Caring in a Congregation

The congregation

The board of deacons or elders

The caring team

The support groups
or the shepherds

The hurting
individual
or
couple

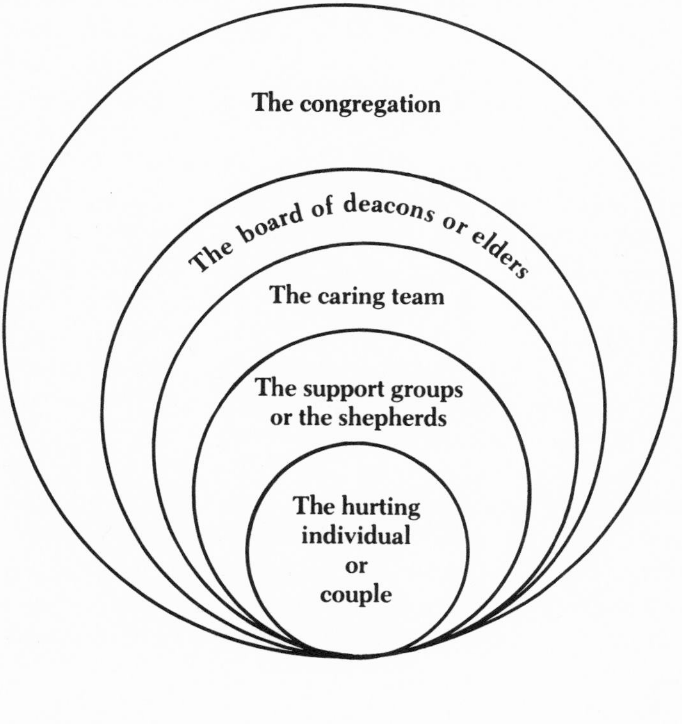

Designated spiritual leaders are known by a variety of names. Here, the term *board of deacons* or *elders* is used. Within the larger circle is a smaller circle which represents this group. The overall task of the board of deacons or elders is to give oversight to all congregational matters that involve worship, faith, and practice. They may also give guidance to matters related to marriages, especially to those marriages which are hurting. The elders, in turn, select another group to deal solely with these latter issues.

The circle within the circle of deacons or elders is designated as the *caring team*. The illustration shows that this group reports directly to the board of elders and is accountable to the elders for all of its actions. The elders, in turn, are accountable to the entire congregation.

Another smaller circle may be drawn to illustrate the role of support groups and shepherds. In the diagram these are shown by dotted lines. A broken line is used to show that these two services are accountable to the caring team only under certain circumstances. They are accountable only when they accept an assignment from the caring team to support or nurture an individual or a couple as part of the caring team's strategy for ministry. In all other aspects of their work they are accountable only to the board of elders or the congregation.

Many congregations have existing *support groups* and all members are encouraged to join. These groups minister to the needs of members, regardless of the nature of the need. If a person in an extreme crisis is seen by the caring team, the utilization of this support group would be encouraged. Persons not members of a support group would be encouraged and assisted in finding such a group.

It needs to be understood that all people really do need a meaningful support group for emotional and spiritual growth. The main task of members of the congregation is to provide support for each other in face-to-face encounters and to invite persons from outside the fellowship to experience this kind of forgiving and affirming support. Support groups also are encouraged to refer situations for which they are not equipped to the caring team.

In some cases a special support group may be created or called upon to work with a specific individual or couple on behalf of the caring team. The caring team may give oversight to the appointment and guidance of this group. In other cases it would be related to a specific problem. For instance, a couple might be devastated by their inability to resolve a matter related to the purchase or sale of real estate. An informed group of congregational members could be called upon to help them evaluate the options of the venture. In the end, the way they work out the solution would be reported to the caring team. At other times individuals may need the help of an ongoing small group to pray with, help, and support them while they go through a particular crisis.

It may also be helpful, at times, to assign a specific person to undertake a *shepherd role* in the life of a hurting person. All members of the congregation are invited to be that caring individual whenever they see a need around them. They are encouraged to lead the hurting person to the caring team and then stand by, on call, if and when their help is needed. At other times, the team may select someone as a shepherd for a specific need. This could be for a person who needs someone available at times of acute crisis, just as the person trying to overcome alcoholism needs an ex-alcoholic available when the temptation to drink is unbearable.

The individual or couple who becomes the concern of the team is represented by the inner smallest circle. The diagram also illustrates that needy persons are encircled by a small group of compassionate, caring, and competent persons who will walk with them on behalf of the congregation through whatever valleys they must go, as well as to celebrate with them whatever mountaintops they experience.

The interrelationship of each of these circles needs to be clearly defined and understood.

The congregation, through the board of elders, gives a

mandate to the team to represent them in all matters pertaining to personal or marital failures. This means the team is responsible to act according to the overall faith and practice of the congregation with each individual or couple, and at the same time to provide whatever process is needed to heal brokenness.

As a method of reporting to the congregation, the caring team should report periodically to the board of elders (or deacons) in the context of confidentiality. Information of the resolution of situations which have become public could be shared. Information on policies which guided the ministry of the caring team could also be reviewed and updated with the elders. Even cases which have not become public may need to be shared with elders for further counsel and guidance, particularly in relation to the guiding policies established by the congregation.

The elders may report the work of the caring team to the congregation, as is appropriate, through regularly established channels (perhaps at a quarterly or annual business meeting).

Members of the congregation may then share their particular concerns or speak with team members. Some actions of the team may affect other members directly, and these members also need to be taken into account. A concern may warrant a meeting with the entire congregation to give opportunity for many feelings to be aired. The meaning of conciliation must be practical at all times, even when it affects an unrelated member.

The entire congregation should be reminded periodically of the obligation to pass information about personal and marital disruptions to team members. Many times members have confidential information about these matters which, under ordinary circumstances, they have no opportunity to share. In a caring community such information should not be passed on as gossip, but directed to a group that has been asked to act redemptively.

In addition, individuals or couples who wish to explore their personal or marital concerns with total confidentiality should be invited to talk directly with any team member.

The relationship with the board of elders is somewhat more public than meeting with an individual team member. But here also there should be complete confidentiality regarding the names of persons interviewed and the content of such meetings. Periodically, a meeting of the caring team with the board of elders may be useful for mutual exploration of the team's function and the overall effect upon the congregation. The board of elders, with its broader view of the congregation in action, may ask the team to assume more or less responsibility, if appropriate. Also, they may correct or enlighten the team about the exact stance of the congregation on specific issues.

A deep trusting relationship should always be present between the team and the pastor(s). Since the pastor, or the pastoral team, is part of the caring team they are fully informed about all team activity. The most crucial issue that always arises is the pastor's willingness to rely on the team for decisions pertaining to the purpose for which it was created. It seems appropriate that the pastor share pertinent information from his private counseling, whether it be individual, premarital, or marital counseling. This does not violate his contract with members if it is understood that he shares openly with the caring group as a normal part of the way he functions in the congregation. Most pastors need a competent support group from within the congregation to help in the oversight and supervision of counseling with persons experiencing critical crises.

There are times when the action taken by an individual, or couple, and the team must be made public. This is an absolute necessity whenever an action becomes a congregational concern.

Prior to the remarriage of a divorced person, it is advisable that a public announcement be made. At times this can be a very brief statement printed in the church bulletin. This should be followed by an invitation to all members to contact team members if they have any question or comments about the action taken.

There is also value, on some occasions, for the pastor or another team member to give a testimonial on behalf of the couple during a Sunday morning worship service and to invite the counsel of members. This makes the team's action more personal and provides an excellent occasion to inform the congregation that the team is still at work even though they may have seen no outward evidence.

A second diagram illustrates another aspect of this model. Figure 2 shows an upright pyramid with a pyramid inverted above, overlapping slightly at the two peaks.

The inverted triangle depicts the congregation at the base and the board of elders at the peak. This diagram illustrates that the work of a large body is delegated to a smaller one.

On the lower triangle, the ongoing support groups are at the base, the hurting persons and couples are next, and the caring team at the peak. The caring team represents the group of persons available to give help.

Figure 2
A Congregational Contract

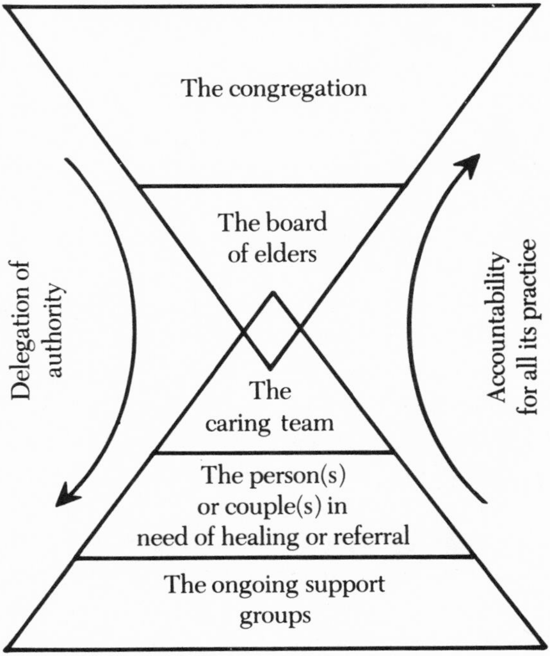

The congregation

The board
of elders

Delegation of
authority

Accountability
for all its practice

The
caring team

The person(s)
or couple(s) in
need of healing or referral

The ongoing support
groups

The pyramids which overlap slightly at the tips illustrate that the board of elders and the caring team are interdependent. Their ties are meaningful, even though the amount or passage of information may be limited.

The arrow on the left indicates that authority for action moves from the congregation downward. The congregation is involved in working with brokenness in persons even though it has delegated the authority to act to a small group. Conversely, the arrow on the right indicates that accountability for all that is done resides ultimately with the congregation. The people in crises are accountable to the team. The team is accountable to the board of elders, and they are accountable to the congregation.

A question remains. How much authority should the team actually have? The answer is simple—as much as the congregation has. Each congregation needs to establish the policies of faith to guide the team in dealing with special needs. One of these is the policy regarding divorce and remarriage. The team then has the authority to function within these guidelines. Such delegation is essential for the team to function effectively. However, this authority must be exercised with utmost love and with respect for the policies of the congregation.

When a caring team has carefuly worked through a problem with persons, they may want to report to the congregation. It would be especially meaningful if persons who have been helped would desire to share their renewed relationship, or a verification of the working of God's grace in their lives, or a new discovery of the healing power of the community of believers. This should be done with a sense of certainty that the action taken by the team is in keeping with God's plan just as much as if the action were the result of congregational consensus. All members need to assume that Christ was present, even as Christ is present in the lives of all disciples who meet and deal prayerfully with issues and relationships of persons in need. A team report should not lead to a congregational vote. But members should have the freedom to question the decision, and the team should be ready to answer. This, too, is part of the entire conciliatory process.

4

How to Begin

How does a team begin? Each congregation must take into account its organizational structure, the role of the pastor, the diversity, the gifts, and the skills of its members. A team also should consider the needs of the congregation, as well as the readiness of the congregation to utilize a team approach in caring for these needs.

More specifically, a team should begin slowly by relating to one situation and remain within its capability in dealing with a particular problem. Then, as the team gains experience in dealing with these situations and feels the leading of the Holy Spirit, they can reach out to more persons or tackle more difficult problems.

The first seed of an eventual caring team may begin with any one who has caught a vison of compassion for hurting persons in the congregation.

Let's assume that you are that person. You notice Susan, who seems to yearn for friendship, and you speak with her. You discover that beneath her sadness Susan is a very troubled person. She is unable to bear the burden of life alone and is slipping into depression. You meet with Susan for lunch and, as soon as you show her that you care, she inundates you with her overwhelming burden. As you listen gently, she feels that you care deeply and unloads more of her burden.

Following this, you felt acutely helpless. After all, what value

was there in your listening to Susan? You did not come up with
any concrete suggestions to help her. You simply did not have any
to offer. You did not even know what the next step might be.
After her request for help, you prayed for her and told her that
you would continue to pray for her during the next weeks.

Much to your surprise, Susan called you the following day to
tell you that she was extremely grateful for your help and that you
have the gift of being a compassionate listener. Susan said that she
was motivated to read a familiar devotional passage and that she
had prayed sincerely for the first time in years. She said that her
greatest reward was that she had slept through the night for the
first time in many months, and that life felt more worthwhile because she felt so rested.

Then Susan asked, "Could we go out for lunch together
regularly?"

At this point, the first phase of beginning a caring team
emerges. You assign to yourself the role of a spiritual friend and
you let her know that she is your very special friend. Next you arrange to meet with her at a time appropriate to both of your
schedules.

At some time, you may want to tell her that you are functioning as a spiritual shepherd to her and that she is your very special
sheep.

It is important that you do not rush beyond this level of functioning. You need to grow. You need to watch another person use
you for their own struggle. You also need to experience yourself
emerging as a helping person over an extended period of time.

Let's continue with the next step. In a church service you
notice Alice seems to be hurting. Instead of approaching her, you
ask Mary, another member, to be a shepherd for Alice. You tell
Mary about the discovery that you have made in your venture
with Susan. Later you and Mary may share your joys and difficulties with each other, and together learn how to be better
shepherds.

Sometime you will want to approach the pastor, or the board
of elders, and tell them about your vision for the congregation.

You may share your experiences with Susan and your vision for a healing team in your congregation, and ask the pastor or elders whether your congregation's structure has a place where such a caring and healing model could be included.

The following questions might be posed to the pastor or elders: (1) Where could we begin? (2) How great is the need? (3) What are our resources?

There are other ways to begin a caring team. If the pastor or official board of the church has caught the vision that more interpersonal care is needed in your congregation, a good first move would be to make a general announcement, or suggest a sermon entitled "Every Member a Priest for the Lord."

Following this, members could be asked to volunteer as shepherds. These persons could go through an initial training program on listening to and caring for hurting individuals.° This would help alert members to those in the congregation who may need a special person to walk with them through a valley which seems too deep to walk through alone. A shepherd group could meet periodically for mutual sharing of their private discoveries about the meaning of shepherding (not gossip sessions), and could eventualy grow into an official caring team.

In most situations of overt sin, a congregation rather quickly comes to the conclusion that a major spiritual change is necessary and a compassionate response comes from various directions. The problem of divorce is not nearly as bothersome to most congregations as the issue of remarriage. The so-called "innocent party" often chooses to remain in the church, and the so-called "guilty party" chooses to leave.

Most congregations know how to care for the hurting and disposed-of mate. However, an honest look at the many young couples and the existing marital separations indicates that the fact of remarriage is not far away.

There comes a time when a clear statement as to exactly

°The book *The Caring Church* by Howard Stone (Philadelphia: Fortress Press, 1983) came to our attention after this book was written. It is an excellent resource for training shepherds or caring persons in the congregation.

where a congregation stands concerning divorce and remarriage must emerge. It is important to go through the full process of a congregational study of divorce and remarriage. Congregations need to define their position, or perhaps incorporate ideas borrowed from other congregations. These statements are usually available from denominational headquarters.

After the study, an official statement of a congregation needs to be prepared. Hopefully, it will emerge heavy on the side of "grace" and light on the side of "judgment." (See Appendix B for a sample statement.)

The final resolution of that statement prepares the way for a caring team to function. "We hereby resolve that it is the responsibility of the congregation to find solutions under God's leading, for every situation that may arise."

What if a congregation simply cannot arrive at the position where they can open the door to remarried persons? Or perhaps more crucially, they cannot see how one of their own members could be divorced and later be helped through a remarriage process by that same body of believers. Does this mean that a caring team cannot work?

In these situations a team can commit itself to dealing with all other crises and simply exclude the divorce issue from its agenda. The couple seeking remarriage can be helped to see that this particular body of believers is not ready to receive them. Naturally that would be a very awkward situation, but it too can be dealt with appropriately.

After the official position of the church is written, the task remains of deciding how this can be implemented into a practical program. The caring team model is one method of approaching this problem.

A caring team could be created and move through several phases of development without the official sanction of the congregation. For some congregations this might be the correct way to proceed.

Most pastors or boards of elders have the right to ask several members of the congregation to encircle a hurting member.

Persons could be asked to support and care for specific persons for a limited period of time. The main purpose, at this level, would be to listen intently and to spend time in mutual prayer and fellowship as they support persons who are going through a particularly painful phase of life.

This group could begin conversing among themselves and agree to move to the next phase. This would mean that they should be elected or appointed by some official body of the congregation.

If the group now feels a sense of call to move ahead, they must carefully assess their gifts and those of the congregation. Is there the right blend of personalities? Are they representative of the entire congregation?

It is essential that a team continue to grow. It is necessary to stop and ask some questions. What is happening to the team? Where did we begin? Where are we presently? In what direction are we moving as a team?

There is yet another way to begin a team approach for caring. This might be called the "high dive" method.

If the church already has a redemptive stance toward all hurting members (including divorce and remarriage), the pastor, board of elders, and the congregation have a clear call to move ahead.

If a congregation has caught the vision of a redeeming fellowship which may delegate some crisis situations to a group of its members, an entire team can be chosen and given a clear mandate to reach out to hurting persons in that congregation. Then it becomes the team's task to make themselves operational.

With such a clear mandate, how does a team begin to function?

A team might begin with some easier tasks such as seeing persons who are experiencing a major transition in life, rather than seeing persons who are experiencing acute crises.

For example, a pastor or board of elders may concur that some premarital couples should be seen by the caring team for four one-hour sessions prior to the wedding. This can be a learning experience for the team to see what it means to meet for an hour with a couple and can help a team understand the nature of its function.

It must be clear why the team meets with couples for premarital counseling. The specific purpose is to help a couple arrive at the altar better prepared for marriage to each other. In most cases this is exacty what would occur. The team members would be able to help a young couple examine aspects of their relationship which had not occurred to them.

The next task of the team would be to share effective ways of dealing with the issues present. The focus should not be to examine the couple's appropriateness for each other. After several sessions, this might evolve as the couple's own conclusion. If this happens, then helping them struggle with those issues could be beyond the capability of a newly organized team. Referral to an outside resource would be a wise course of action, with an invitation to return to the team at a later time, either individually or jointly.

A team who has several years of experience might be prepared to take on the challenge of working through a decision about the wisdom of continuing a problematic courtship.

An excellent beginning task for a team would be to meet with an older dating couple who was married previously and their mates had died. Usually counseling with couples like these is an enjoyable task from whom a team can learn and gain experience. Since there is no moral question involved, it would also give a team member the opportunity to make a wedding announcement to the congregation. Through this the congregation would see how the team works, and its purpose. The message would be conveyed to the congregation that the team is available for anyone who may need it.

John, a regional bishop, heard about the model and was eager to implement the team approach. In reviewing his situation he realized that he served six medium-sized congregations in a rural area. He concluded that none of the congregations could begin a caring team of their own because of a lack of resources. In analyzing the situation, John was certain that he understood the team approach and concluded that he had the gift to give it direction. In addition he had spent time with Peter, a psychologist who was a member of one of the congregations, processing ideas about how the church could utilize Peter's gifts and skills. John decided to begin by asking Peter for help to conceptualize the idea and become a member of the future team. John then concluded that a single team could serve all six congregations, with the team to include a lay delegate and either an elder, or a pastor, from each of the congregations. If a couple or individual with a special relationship with their home pastor were to be seen, that pastor would be asked to be present even though he was not a member of the permanent team. John was not certain what the future direction would be, but at least he saw the beginning step.

The impetus which gave John a sense of urgency should have been a cause for joy to any congregation, but there was a hidden pain. The congregations for which he was responsible were remarkably effective in bringing adult families from the community into their congregations. The hidden pain was that divorce and remarriage were part of the past of many of these membership candidates. The congregations had tried not to pay too much attention to this, but all of the pastors had communicated their concern that "looking the other way" was not the answer. The older original members also had expressed concern that, in some way, a clearer message should be given that these congregations take a very "high view" of marriage. Yet, at the same time, they wanted to clearly show that grace and accountability must be the message of the body of believers.

The last illustration shows an innovative approach to the model. It takes into account the unique problems and then molds the model to fit the problems.

The whole question of how to begin must be faced with a clear awareness of the uniqueness of every situation. It must be seen as an evolving process, both for the team and for the congregation. The team should not allow itself to be pushed to move beyond its readiness by a particular crisis. This may mean that another resource must be found, or another direction must be followed in certain situations.

Finally, it is important to test the leading of the Lord in the beginning process. Prayer and searching for direction under God's guidance is essential. Crisis situations requiring careful processing and persons prepared to serve in a special way are clear signals that a group of believers who proclaim renewal, redemption, and reconciliation need to respond.

5

The Emerging Caring Team

It will take years for a caring team to grow to an advanced level of functioning. In a sense a team never stops growing. No two persons or problems are the same. This, in itself, forces a team to develop new strategies and find new responses. With the replacement of each team member, the composition of the team changes. As new gifts are added, a new style emerges.

The evolution of the first caring team in which we participated is a story of its own. In the congregation, where we were members, we saw the need for a response to acute hurts and brokenness.

More than ten years ago an elder statesman of our denomination spent a year as a resource leader for our congregation. Among the many studies he led was one on the issue of divorce and remarriage. The congregation was open to being redemptive since grace was a major belief of our denomination. When the question of accountability arose, the congregation did not desire a "closed eyes" policy toward all divorce and remarriage.

At that point we suggested a team approach to deal with each couple who had been divorced and was seeking the sanction of the congregation for remarriage. Then, a team was appointed by the elders, called The *Divorce and Remarriage Committee*. It had one task—to be a gatekeeper for remarriage applicants. The elders asked the committee to continue in dialogue with applicants for remarriage for as long as was needed to convince the committee (1) that this remarriage was in keeping with a spiritually redemptive process, (2) that there was an emotionally healthy relationship, (3) and that there was agreement with the wishes of this particular congregation.

After a number of years the assignment was enlarged and the name of the group was then changed to the *Marital Reconciliation Committee.* Reconciliation was defined to include intervention in any way which would bring wholeness to situations where there was brokenness in marriage. In addition, troubled courtships were included, even though no divorce was involved. Support was also offered to individuals whose spouses threatened divorce.

As the years passed, new pastors worked with the team as others left the congregation. Time was needed to orient each new pastor to this style of relating to crises in marriage. Also the pastor, as a team member, presented additional issues for the committee's consideration. The committee became a forum for the pastor to process his own feelings about troubling situations in the congregation.

The next major move came years later when the name of the group was changed to *Counseling Ministry Team,* and the scope broadened to include any crisis situation which might emerge. When it became inappropriate for the team to deal with a situation, individuals were guided to seek help from a resource outside the congregation.

This time schedule is not necessarily an ideal one. Since there was no model to follow, the team had to develop methods to deal with crisis situations as they arose. We suggest that a team be permitted to emerge so that learning will occur from both the victories and the failures.

To conceptualize how the growth process can evolve, refer to Figure 3, a diagram on the emerging growth of the team. Although we have listed an assumed gradation of sixteen transitional or crisis situations which a congregation may face, there may be many more. Generally, they are listed in order of difficulty for the team to encounter. All situations have their own unique built-in

Figure 3
The Emerging Growth of the Caring Team

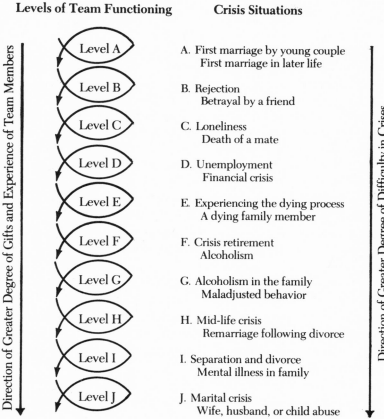

Levels of Team Functioning   **Crisis Situations**

Direction of Greater Degree of Gifts and Experience of Team Members

Level A — A. First marriage by young couple
First marriage in later life

Level B — B. Rejection
Betrayal by a friend

Level C — C. Loneliness
Death of a mate

Level D — D. Unemployment
Financial crisis

Level E — E. Experiencing the dying process
A dying family member

Level F — F. Crisis retirement
Alcoholism

Level G — G. Alcoholism in the family
Maladjusted behavior

Level H — H. Mid-life crisis
Remarriage following divorce

Level I — I. Separation and divorce
Mental illness in family

Level J — J. Marital crisis
Wife, husband, or child abuse

Direction of Greater Degree of Difficulty in Crises

variables. What on the surface appears to be a simple first courtship and marriage for a young couple may turn out to be an acutely difficult situation involving infidelity, premarital pregnancy, and whatever may accompany it.

A team should begin with the most simple situations and move on to the more difficult ones as it gains skill and experience.

In the diagram this is illustrated by a series of interlocking circles which are identified by the letters from A to J. These circles identify the level at which a particular team is prepared to function. This is shown to underscore the absolute necessity for a team to evaluate itself and its own level of functioning. The team must repeatedly ask itself whether to accept or continue to deal with a particular situation.

A number of known variables determine the level of functioning for a particular team. The first has been referred to before—the age and experience of the team. If a team is growing, it will proceed beyond the first situations to more difficult tasks.

"What are the unique skills and gifts present in a team?" is a question that must be faced to determine the role and direction of growth of the team.

If the pastor has the gift of counseling, it will add to the depth of the encounters. If the pastor has special training or may be in a clinical pastoral education program, he can use his own training program to test out the appropriateness for the team to be involved, or present situations from the team for supervision in that program.

If the team has a trained counselor member, this too will affect the depth of involvement. In most cases the added skills brought by gifted and trained members will give the team confidence to deal with more difficult crisis situations.

A team should also have the freedom to decide to remain within an appropriate range of services. This could be based on the time and energy which they have available for this task. The trained counselor may choose to be used in a limited way, and refer complicated situations to resources outside the congregation.

A team may continue to be involved in a complicated crisis far beyond their ability. The key in such a situation is to tell the individuals that the team chooses to continue, although it is a situation in which the team is unable to bring the needed resolution. However, the team should not pretend to be more skillful than it really is. An honest counselor admits that, at times, there is an inability to know the next move, but there is trust that a light may dawn later, or that a breakthrough may occur which will bring hope and greater healing.

The meeting with the team is a special time set aside to listen to the pain, to permit tears to be shed, to hold hands in prayer, and to promise to remember individuals with needs in private prayer frequently. The only promise a team should make to individuals who seek help is that it will walk with them, prayerfully, through whatever valley may be encountered. The team offers help to the degree that it is capable at each phase and no more.

Here is a situation in which a team was severely tested. It illustrates how important it is that a team define its role and follow its mandate even under great pressure.

George, a man in his mid-thirties, had lived most of his adult life out of fellowship with the congregation, although he was on the membership list. Since he traveled far and wide, members of the congregation knew little about his lifestyle, and less about his faith. George's parents remained active in the congregation but said little about him.

One day George appeared at the pastor's study with Nancy, a young woman who was twice divorced, requesting the pastor to marry them within a month in the church. George assumed a right to all of the church's facilities because he was a member, even though he had not attended in his adult life.

When the pastor explained the policy of the congregation and mentioned the work of the team, George hardly batted an eye. He restated his demand and threatened to confront anyone who opposed his demands. However, the pastor was able to arrange a meeting of George and Nancy with the caring team.

At the first meeting George stated his wishes emphatically, and was derogatory toward any team member who questioned his intentions. He told the team that he was bargaining only for the right to use the building and for the pastor's service to perform the ceremony. In no way was he attempting to be reconciled to the congregation or to Christ as its Head. George brought up the old argument about all the hypocrites in the congregation, and said that in no way would he go along with them.

A woman on the team leaned toward George. Quietly, but kindly and with authority, she explained the meaning of their congregation, its belief in the forgiving power of Christ, and the way the caring team was formed to further this process. George was completely overwhelmed. After a few moments of stuttering, he exclaimed that he already had another pastor who was willing to perform the ceremony, so all he needed was the building. The team then told him it was available to anyone for the asking. He simply needed to schedule it. The team assured George that this was not their concern, but added that his attitudes bothered them much. He was told that as a member of that congregation he could not proceed as he intended without jeopardizing his membership. He replied, "Then I'll have it removed." A team member asked, "Do you really mean that?" It was suggested that if he did, then he should state the request in writing, and he would then be dealt with. In anger, he asked for a sheet of paper.

Another team member suggested that the group form a circle and all hold hands for prayer. The couple was included in the circle and the prayers by team members were personal and filled with compassion. When the prayers ended Nancy was in tears, and George was choking back emotion. For the first time he was touched by "tough love." This was new to him. George asked for directions as to how to proceed with arrangements for the use of the church building for their wedding.

It will take years of growth for a team to arrive at the readiness to deal with such an episode with clarity and maturity. It is important that the caring team and the task of the team be viewed as an evolving process so it becomes more effective. This is similar to an effective counselor who must aways keep growing in order to facilitate others to grow. With each stage of growth, the helper becomes more capable of aiding more troubled persons.

A team must always be aware of their level of competence or incompetence. To respond when they are able, to refer when they are not, is essential. To know when to act, and when not to act, comes with the maturing of the team as a healing arm of a congregation.

6

Healing Skills

Skills are required to respond effectively to a diversity of persons. Team members bring their own innate skills of relating to people. Some of these skills are learned in early childhood as others cared for them. Other skills are developed through interpersonal relationships as adolescents, or during a courtship and marriage process. Then there are the skills which are discovered by caring for hurting persons both within and beyond the family. Many of the growth-oriented self-help books now on the market teach effective interpersonal skills and have been read by many persons. The main thrust of all education in counseling is focused on training for skills. To whatever degree team members have utilized these resources, they will have gained knowledge of specifically defined skills for helping others.

Many authorities in the field say it is possible for friends and relatives to provide healing which is equal to, or even better than, that which can be provided by counselors or therapists in certain specific situations.

Because of the absence of really caring persons, the absence of an available kinship system, and the loss of a viable community, gradually people have turned to paid counselors to obtain the caring they need but are unable to find in their environment. Sometimes, psychotherapy is referred to as purchased love. We suggest that it is possible to gather together many helpful skills in a congregation, or a group of congregations, to freely dispense healing love and also fulfill the calling of the congregation to be a caring community.

The following skills are important so they will be defined. In addition, examples will be included which show when these skills may be used and why it is necessary to use them.

1. *Loving.* In this setting we define love as "the choice to be for another person what that person needs us to be, without counting the cost to ourselves." This is our attempt to take Christ's statement and make it operational today: "Greater love has no one than this, that one lay down his life for his friends" (John 15:13).

The problem with the statement Christ used is that few people are ever called upon to choose the lives of others over their own lives. Since usually that is not the option, then how does one exercise love?

Using that same concept, there are many situations where one can choose to love or not to love. The choice depends on one's willingness to see what another really needs from us . What are we to be for another? With a clear awareness that there is a price to pay, one can choose to pay that price so that the needs of another are met. Ultimately, that is putting love into practice.

The art of loving is a skill which must overshadow all others. The congregation, as Christ's body in a particular location, must see loving as its highest calling. After all, Jesus defined himself and God the Father as being best experienced by the exercise of love. If this is who God is, then this is what the congregation must exemplify in all its actions including the work of the caring team.

The exercise of love is put to a severe test when someone in the congregation is defiantly sinning. It is even more difficult to love when an arrogant attitude and an absence of penitence is associated with this behavior. Even in the midst of such situations, a caring team needs to truly love.

2. *Confronting.* Although confronting is a useful skill, we need to be aware of the danger of destructive confrontation. Examples of congregational committees who faced erring mem-

bers and then proceeded to enlighten the erring ones on the standards of the church are numerous. Many times this has resulted in requesting persons to terminate membership. Too often the confrontation between the official congregational representative or group and the erring member has left deep scars.

In a recent situation a church official requested an individual not to participate in the upcoming communion service because of what others viewed as unbecoming behavior. The official representative called the erring member by phone to tell him about this decision. The erring member was given no opportunity to defend his position, which he said differed greatly from the way it was viewed by others.

The model of a caring team suggests that there is a need for confrontation in vital issues such as a violation of the faith and practice of the congregation. This may, in the end, result in a request that the violator forego communion, or even terminate membership. The crucial difference from the previous illustration is that the caring team should engage an erring member in a redemptive process, with the unfailing desire to restore such a person to full fellowship. This can be done in a gentle caring way without condoning the wrong. The sin needs to be defined and explicitly spelled out. Then the caring team needs to invite the erring member to join in a redemptive journey in which team members become partners in the search for healing and wholeness.

Let's assume that a young couple is living together without having taken the marriage vows, but they wish to continue in full fellowship with the church. A caring team would face the issue of "morality in changing times" and "everybody else is doing it." This need not derail the team. They can adhere to the simple biblical position and the standards of the congregation while they deal with the couple. This couple could be referred to a counselor for a period of premarital counseling and then report back to the team. The key is to communicate a depth of compassion to the couple as they struggle with their decision. There is a clear goal in mind that the couple finally choose marriage, or else choose to live apart to remain in full fellowship with the congregation.

In most instances, people in predicaments like these are grateful for a group of fellow members to enter into the struggle with them. Usually, they also are experiencing acute guilt and frustration and do not know how to resolve their dilemma. When a caring team is available, they find help for situations they are unable to handle alone.

We strongly recommend that people be dealt with gently. The more crucial the crisis, the more soft the gloves need to be. This can be done even in the face of immorality and sin.

The real value of a team functioning in this type of situation is that a group of persons can prevent any one team member from acting out his own unconscious fears or hatred toward certain deviant behavior.

If a team member feels vulnerable to a particular situation, because of the nature of the problem or the closeness to a situation, at times it may be necessary to withdraw from participation. Then a temporary replacement may be selected (if needed) to serve so that a caring team can be more redemptive in a particular situation.

3. *Freeing.* Many people bear burdens which should not be theirs to carry. Some are overwhelmed with guilt that is not their own. Such persons often can do nothing about a situation, yet they hold themselves accountable. Someone needs to tell them that this is false guilt. It is a false burden and a false bondage. For these persons, false guilt feels the same as if they were truly guilty, but in these situations it is only a feeling. These persons have done no wrong. They need to be told that they have not erred so that the weight of that burden can be left behind. A team of fellow Christians from their own congregation are in a position to call it a faulty load and thus free the persons from this burden.

Beverly was overcome by the weight of her parents' troubled marriage. Throughout her childhood, and even as an adult, she had seen her parents battering each other for years. As an only child, Beverly could never separate what was her task or what was her parents' task, since she had no siblings with whom to test her feelings. In addition, each parent baited her into the crises. At each round of events she could expect two telephone calls, two stories, and two people pleading for her loyalty.

By the time Beverly turned to the caring team, the problems had already affected her marriage, as well as her children. All were quite weary of seeing her drawn into every fight and then devastated with helplessness. Also there was a nagging sense of guilt that listening to one parent was always a betrayal of the other parent.

The caring team quickly identified that Beverly was carrying a burden that did not belong to her. She was not obligated to forsake her own family to respond to her parents. Worse, her involvements with her parents did not help them and might even harm them. Beverly's assumption that she needed to be involved out of Christian compassion was wrong.

Beverly's parents needed professional counseling. A team member gave her the name of a competent counselor and advised her to keep reminding her parents that she would no longer assume that role and that they must turn to an appropriate resource. In addition, Beverly was advised to tell them that her involvement was wrong for them as parents, for her as a child, and for her role as a wife and mother. "So it is wrong, wrong, wrong, and it cannot continue."

Then the team helped Beverly free herself of false guilt. Beverly could understand that, as an only child, it would seem necessary to assume responsibility for her parents' behavior, since she had been baited into this role from early childhood. It was a lifelong lesson that she had learned. Beverly also acknowledged that she was extremely susceptible to other persons' suggestions. Now she realized that she needed to switch the source of suggestion about what was right for her to do from her parents to her own family and to the caring team. Also the team assured her that they would be her family in Christ and the brothers and sisters which she never had.

4. *Processing.* At times the most important task of a caring team is simply to process what is brought to them. By processing we mean that the team members engage in reflective listening,

making certain (1) that they understand everything which is being said, (2) that they clarify what they think is being said, and (3) that they call attention to issues that are involved which are not being faced. In the end, the caring team only summarizes the content of the session and offers their prayer support. This leaves the individuals to struggle with the crisis for several weeks and then return to engage the team in a continuation of the search. This skill should be utilized to some degree in every session.

Processing, rather than solving problems, avoids taking responsibility for life's journey away from the person. In reality, any individual seeking help should be guided to own the problem, own the healing experience and, in the end, own the outcome. The key to accomplishing this is to avoid giving quick and easy answers when the individual really needs to grow by a personal search for answers. Walking with someone is the goal, rather than arriving at a destination. Why should a team assume that their collective wisdom must provide an answer when there is none? It is sufficient to engage someone in a dialogue as he or she is helped to become involved deeper and deeper in the search.

Frequently, it is advisable to avoid the possibility of a wrong solution for an individual's problem by interrupting and ending a session with a summary of what has been said in that particular session. Attention needs to be called to the issues upon which that person needs to do more thinking and arrangements made for the next session. This permits everyone to live with the issues until the next meeting when it may be evident that time has shed some new light on the issues.

Only time and experience will convince a caring team that processing was helpful, although no final solution was found. It is actually advisable for a team to clearly agree that they do not have to bring every situation to a neat ending. Good answers are not necessary. In many situations, answers are not helpful. Often, discovering the right strategy for walking with someone offers more help.

5. *Guiding.* Anna, an elderly widow, came to the attention of the team. Anna's granddaughter and her boyfriend came to visit

at her apartment in a retirement center many months ago. The visit turned out to be indefinite since these young persons actually had no place to live, nor could they afford any. They had no steady employment. Sometimes they left for long periods of time, but they always found their way back when they needed food and shelter.

At the center, short visits were permitted by the administration. However, it was a definite violation for unrelated adults to share a bedroom and remain indefinitely. The young couple persuaded Anna not to tell anyone, and they cautiously eluded the staff. Anna was especially concerned about how to handle the situation since this granddaughter had always been a favorite one and she did not wish to offend her. Anna chose to request them to leave by herself but she was at a loss on to how to do it tactfully.

The caring team guided her through a careful series of strategies which met all of the conditions that the situation required until Anna finally succeeded in getting the couple to leave without creating hard feelings. This process took many weeks as Anna used the team to reflect on how to proceed with each step. Often she needed help to word the exact phrase which she would use to convey her message.

6. *Praying.* Prayer must be an essential ingredient of all of the caring team's activity. Since the team becomes involved in such delicate situations, it is important to call upon God for guidance. Lives, marriages, and families are at stake in each move that is made. Some decisions will have far-reaching effects. It is vital to commit all of this to God's care.

Sometimes the team is totally helpless. In such instances it is appropriate to tell the hurting person that there is a higher power upon which the team calls for help, even though the team may not be able to offer other assistance or direction.

A team that met following a regular morning worship service found themselves in that exact predicament. A public announcement had been made to the congregation that the caring team was available for anyone to drop in if they felt the need. Carol, a young woman who appeared to be deeply distressed, stopped by.

She told them that her younger brother had been caught in an illegal drug operation and was being held as a suspect in a ring that could involve many other people. Carol did not want this to be general knowledge because of the danger to her brother. As a result, she could not ask the congregation for prayer. The caring team realized that Carol needed prayer and that this request could be shared only with a group that knew how to handle confidentiality. First, the team asked Carol to tell about the events leading to the arrest, exactly·what her brother meant to her, and how she was affected by these events. After Carol talked about it, she seemed relieved. Then the group formed a circle with her, holding hands as they prayed for her and for her brother, as well as for the authorities involved. Carol also prayed, eloquently pleading for God's wisdom as she related to her brother. Other skills were later used in dealing with Carol but, at this moment, prayer was essential.

Loving, confronting, freeing, processing, guiding, and praying are only six of the crucial skills which the caring team must exercise. Many more could be included, such as:

Listening—the art of sensitively tuning-in to the words that people are saying or trying to say.°

Sharing—the ability to pass on to each other experiences which help clarify the issues under discussion.

Waiting—the willingness not to push persons beyond what they can handle and to give them the time they need to struggle alone with a problem.

Bearing—offering to get under the load that others are carrying without feeling overloaded.

Advising—the capacity to draw upon one's own wisdom and apply it to another's problem.

Modeling—the skill of demonstrating an attribute which another needs to learn, such as being sensitive when sensitivity is the attribute which another person needs to manifest.

°See *The Art of Listening with Love* by Abraham Schmitt (Nashville: Abingdon Press, 1982) for more on listening.

Touching—the readiness to put one's arm around a hurting person in order to physcially communicate support.

Reflecting—the ability to play back verbally what another is saying so that it can be viewed more clearly from several vantage points.

A caring team must be flexible and resourceful in its use of all the strategies which they can discover to enable them to bring healing and wholeness to the lives of others.

7

The Team in Action

It would be helpful to permit the reader to experience a number of examples of the team in action. This will show the diversity of the problems that may be encountered and the need for creating unique strategies to fit each situation. The goal is to achieve reconciliation between persons.

Illustration one. The pastor reported briefly on the welfare of a troubled couple who had accepted his suggestion to secure marriage counseling help at a center which the team had recommended. The pastor continued to meet frequently with the husband who asked for help for his own spiritual growth. This had become a tutoring arrangement in which the pastor gave extensive reading assignments for joint discussion at the next session. The husband felt a need for contact with the pastor, and the pastor expressed satisfaction in this arrangement and also gratitude to the team for preventing him from slipping into a counselor role.

Illustration two. On this occasion the team met in the living room of a team member, because her home is located between the homes of two congregational members who asked for this meeting.

One of the individuals owns a corporation and the other person is director of personnel at this firm. Their concern involved an employee who should be fired if good labor practices were to be followed. However, they found this prospect difficult because they wished to respond as Christ would want them to. They knew the enormous consequences this would have for the employee and his family. To terminate his employment seemed cruel. When the two reflected on other options open to them, involving the caring team was suggested by one. This seemed appropriate since the two office staff members and the employee were all members of a congregation where there was an existing team. It seemed appropriate to turn to the team because the employee was loudly accusing them of arrogant and uncharitable behavior, instead of looking at his own unacceptable conduct.

Fortunately, they had informed the employee that they were turning to the caring team for arbitration. All agreed that the outcome of the team process would be acceptable and binding in the employment settlement and that no recriminations would follow. The employee agreed to refrain from any public accusations, and the employer would also keep all matters confidential.

After the entire story was told by the management, the team accepted the assignment requesting that the employer and personnel director return to work and explain their decision to the employee who was to call any team member to set up a time for meeting.

Since the caring team was equipped to deal with stressful interpersonal relations it was also their commitment to accept situations involving their members that occur entirely outside of the congregation. If a situation should arise where only one person was a member of the congregation, they would be ready to respond to see if a reconciling process could be devised.

Illustration three. The pastor reported that Allen was waiting to meet with the team. He briefly told the team that Allen had been divorced by his wife about a year ago, and that he had been a member of the adult inquirers' class, with the intention of being received into church membership. Although the pastor had seen him in individual pastoral counseling and also in class, he did not feel right recommending him for membership at this time. He had told Allen that the caring team would meet with him since there had been a divorce in his life.

As Allen entered the room, he expressed eagerness to meet with the team. He was grateful for the compassion he had felt in the congregation.

As Allen related his story, many other messages came through. He was a thoroughly confused and lonely person who had been unable to bring any part of his life into focus. Now, he was grasping at straws, of which this congregation was one. Remarriage was on his mind to the extent that it appeared to dominate most of the decisions in his life. It seemed apparent to the team that Allen saw church membership as a way of raising his eligibility for a successful courtship. Various team members expressed their concern that he had his priorities jumbled, and that this was an inappropriate time to make a decision on membership. Allen understood this, but was somewhat shocked that this was so obvious to the group.

The team then made a series of recommendations. First, Allen was asked to delay his request for membership for one year, during which time he should repeat the membership class. He was not very well acquainted with the congregation and knew little about the doctrine and the commitment of the denomination. Allen's mind seemed to have been preoccupied with the eligible women in the congregation who would care for him, as he felt his wife never had, and as the pastor had cared for him in the sessions with him.

Next Allen was asked to relate more closely to the congregation by attending services regularly, joining one of the Sunday school classes, and participating more frequently in church-sponsored social events. The team told him, "Just get to know us as people and stop glamorizing us. We want to know you as a person, too, not just as a discarded divorced individual."

Since the congregation had active support groups, the team gave Allen the name of a person to contact for joining a group appropriate to his need. A year later, the team would ask the support group whether Allen had found himself spiritually.

Allen was told about a local congregation which sponsored a singles' fellowship which he could use to discover the meaning of singleness, and that singleness was an option that needed to be explored as a possible right choice for him. This fellowship would provide a social outlet, as well as diminish his excessive desperation for marriage. The overall message given was, "Let us help you make peace with your divorce and discover a meaningful single life. After that, you may be ready to consider meaningful membership and possible remarriage, but not now."

Individual team members assured Allen that they personally wanted to touch base with him as they met in routine congregational life, and perhaps join him for coffee. He was also given the opportunity to call any of them when he needed to talk.

Allen's final response was, "My, you people really do care what happens to me and you don't waste any time letting me know that I need to get my life together. I do need a lot of help and I accept your recommendations."

Illustration four. On this occasion the team was meeting for the second time with three couples from a young adult Sunday school class. The couples reported that they could not tolerate the outspoken and, in their opinion, disruptive behavior of another couple in the study process. They were on the verge of joining another class and considered attending another congregation. However, this was an unsatisfactory option, since they had developed a close kinship with many of the other class members.

After attempting to talk to the other couple and to many other class members, they continued to be frustrated and finally turned to the team for help.

Prior to this meeting the team had met several times with the couple who were defined as "the culprits." This proved to be very painful for everyone, but the couple agreed to cooperate with the team in its efforts to resolve the problem. The couple used the meetings with the team to air their many bad feelings about being misunderstood and shunned. There was validity to much of what they said, but they also could understand that their behavior contributed to the ill will. It was really a vicious cycle that had gained momentum until someone had to stop it.

In this session the three couples examined what they had

contributed to the disruption, and in what respects the other couple had misunderstood them.

It was now agreed that the next step in the reconciliation process was for the three couples and the other couple to meet as a group with the team. Together they would attempt to work through all the hurts, with the goal of full restoration of the relationship. Since the entire class had become embroiled in the crisis, one team member offered to meet with all of them and openly explain the redemptive process as well as to deal with any loose ends which might remain within the entire class.

This situation illustrates the need for a forum within the congregation where conflicts can be faced and worked at in an orderly way. A caring team may accept this as one of its tasks.

Illustration five. On another occasion a team member reported on his attempt to meet with a young childless couple who had separated within the first year of marriage. These two people were the children of long-term members in the congregation. The parents had made several requests to have the team attempt to intervene. It had been decided earlier that one team member stood the best chance in making the contact, but it proved fruitless. The young husband told him that he did not want anyone meddling in his private life. He had already suspected that the team would approach him, so he was ready for the telephone call.

The team did not have an effective strategy to suggest at this time. The same team member volunteered to talk to the parents periodically to see if there was any decrease in animosity. He also needed to assure the couple that the team had not forgotten them.

It was emphasized to this couple that if they proceeded with divorce action without involving the team they would eventually forfeit their church membership. The item was tabled for later review, since no immediate action was appropriate.

Illustration six. The professional counselor in the group reported that she had had a good session with Sally, a young woman who was present at an earlier team meeting. It had come to the attention of the pastor that Sally was living a life which was out of keeping with the behavior of a Christian. The counselor had volunteered to contact her about this matter. Sally's response was positive in that she accepted the counselor's invitation to meet in her private office.

Sally admitted that her life was really falling apart on many fronts, and she needed help. However, she asked to meet with the counselor rather than the team. She even offered to pay for her own counseling. The counselor accepted this arrangement on the condition that she be given the right to tell the team about it. At a later date, the counselor would also report the outcome of the counseling process to the team.

Illustration seven. At one meeting of the team the pastor reported that he had received a request from Tom, a middle-aged man who, with his *fiancée* Eileen, desired to meet with the team. Tom said he wanted the approval of the team, and thus of the congregation, for his scheduled remarriage. The pastor could have invited Tom and Eileen to be present at the meeting, but he felt sufficiently uncomfortable about this situation that he wanted to meet with the team before he invited Tom and Eileen.

Tom had attended this congregation intermittently for several years with Sally, his first wife, and four adolescent children. Members of the congregation found Sally and the children easy to relate to, but Tom was aloof and often arrogant. Neither Tom nor Sally became members. Suddenly, Tom began divorce proceedings after he became involved with Eileen, a younger single woman who was a marginal church attender and not a member. It was known that Tom had caused a lot of pain to Sally and the children. Eileen's parents had grave doubts about this courtship. They were members of another congregation of the same denomination, and had contacted their pastor about Tom's intentions. Eileen's parents felt that Tom had so overwhelmed their daughter that she was incapable of making a responsible decision.

As the team discussed the situation they were confused about the true intent of Tom's request. Tom did not appear to be honestly seeking help from the team to conduct his courtship and imminent marriage in a way that was pleasing to God and acceptable to the congregation. The team continued to ask questions of each other. What is Tom's real motive? Does he expect the team to give immediate sanction to his destructive behavior to Sally and the children? Is he honestly looking for a redemptive path? Might he be trying to use the team to gain some respectability in the eyes of Eileen's parents? Or was Tom trying to convey a message to his future in-laws that he was complying with the congregation's method of dealing with this situation, using the team to convince them to accept his tactics and accept him as a future son-in-law?

After a few minutes, it was apparent that in not knowing Tom's true intentions, the team could not respond to him at this time.

The trained counselor volunteered an alternative. Rather than asking the couple to meet with the team, she suggested that she meet privately with Tom, and then have several sessions with Tom and Eileen together. In this way she could discover what their real intentions were. After that, she would report to the team. It was just too troubling a situation. The counselor could best face these issues in private sessions, rather than giving Tom a forum to continue an apparently destructive course of action. The team agreed that the pastor should call Tom and ask him to contact the counselor for a series of preliminary sessions before the team would respond to him.

The issue that this team faced was that by establishing a method for responding to divorce and remarriage they were vulnerable to abuse by shrewd or crafty persons who were capable of misusing this method for their own gain. Thus the intent of the congregation would be totally violated. Often pastors find themselves caught in impossible predicaments without a forum to test true intentions. Before a clear perspective emerges, pastors may be drawn into situations which are beyond their ability to handle well.

At this point the team member who also served on the board of deacons suggested that she make a visit to the home of Tom's former wife, Sally, to express the team's concern for what was happening to her. The team agreed to let her know that she would not be abandoned, and needed a true reading of how she was experiencing this divorce proceeding. The counselor concurred that this was an excellent strategy and that she would like to tell Tom that these visits with Sally were part of the team's process. A team needs to respond to all hurting parties in an appropriate way. In this case Sally and the children should not be overlooked.

The pastor stated his desire to contact Eileen's pastor to explain the process of this team so her pastor could assure Eileen's parents that this congregation was not blindly giving a stamp of approval to just any type of divorce and remarriage process.

Illustration eight. At one meeting of the team, Jane, a team member, gave a follow-up report on an assignment she accepted at the previous meeting. It was then apparent that Bob and Ellen, a young couple, were in the throes of an acute marital flare-up. The decision had been made that Jane should make a personal contact with Ellen. Jane followed-up with a telephone call and invited Ellen out for lunch. In the course of this encounter, Ellen expressed her concern about the marriage crisis and was startled that people knew that she was so devastated by the threatening divorce.

The team was told that the visit was received with surprising goodwill. Ellen was shocked that word had reached the team, since she thought it had remained with the several people in whom she had confided. Ellen admitted that she had hit an extreme low as a result of her husband's indifference, but he had partly heard her cry for help and was trying to respond. The couple had explored several options, one of which was to seek private marriage counseling, or to come together to the team and use them to assess the whole situation. The final choice was to try to work it out on their own, since they had already made a small breakthrough. However, Ellen accepted Jane's invitation to meet again in a month or two to reassess the situation.

After the team heard the report they made a number of other

suggestions, but they postponed any further discussion until a second visit.

Illustration nine. An elderly widow asked to meet with the team. She said that slanderous gossip about her had been spread though the congregation and in the community. At the meeting, she tearfully recounted the items as she knew them and what she conjectured people were saying. She was extremely distressed, since the gossip was so unlike the life she had lived and the way she perceived herself. She was encouraged to tell the story about the years of her marriage, about her children who were residing in distant places, and finally about the loss of her husband. After completing the narration of events, she showed a lot of relief. It even appeared that the report of the gossip had lost some of its importance and her need to be understood by someone took precedence.

Since there appeared to be some question about what she considered to be malicious gossip, the pastor suggested that she return to the next meeting of the team rather than confronting the supposed "villain," as she had earlier requested. She was quite grateful that the team took time to listen to her.

After she left the room, the team reviewed their strategy. Everyone had the sense that the gossip issue was not the real agenda. Rather, her life of loneliness was getting to her, and whatever she had heard had been greatly exaggerated as she mulled over it in her isolation. The team members agreed to search for ways to assist her in dealing with her aloneness and then to share these options with her at their next meeting.

These situations are given to illustrate that a caring team must be ready to care genuinely for any person who asks to meet with them. The essence of caring is to be present for the other's need. To listen lovingly to anyone, and to accept whatever deep feelings a person shares, has validity. The ways persons think and behave must be understood, but also they may be challenged.

The examples also demonstrate the need to select the best strategy for responding to crisis situations. Sometimes all that is necessary, or even all that can be done, is to be fully present and listen carefully. At other times, the strategy must be the exact opposite in that an individual needs to be helped to face error. This may be necessary because of the effect it has on other people, or because of failure in living the Christian life or in understanding the life of the community of believers. In some instances a series of sessions is appropriate to experience the issue over an extended time or to explore the effect it has on other persons.

If genuine love dominates the actions of the team, then whatever crisis it faces, the outcome will be beneficial.

8

The Caring Team:
Who and Why

A caring team represents the congregation in helping troubled persons go through crises. The congregation is composed of a group of persons who receive power, through the Holy Spirit, to work toward emotional and spiritual healing for its own members and others who seek for it in the congregation. The congregation is unique as an organization in that members are God's servants completing his work on earth. Members feed the hungry for God, since God does not literally feed them. They also visit prisons on God's behalf. However, there are special areas of need where members individually or as a large group are unable to act effectively. The caring team is a resource within the congregation which ministers on its behalf to these special needs.

When a team approach is adopted there is a major change in the role of the pastor. A pastor is no longer viewed as the primary congregational counselor. Some counseling shifts from the pastor's office to the team. The pastor, as part of the team, remains close to the healing process, but he no longer is solely responsible for all counseling.

David and Vera Mace have made the following statement concerning the role of pastors in marriage counseling:

> Pastors have inevitably been compelled to get into this, and some have taken extensive training in the field. The more we consider the

situation of the churches, the more we have become convinced that the average pastor should not attempt marriage and family counseling, except in the preliminary stages, when his objective should be to get those concerned referred, as quickly as possible, to the competent community agencies that now exist in the field. Marriage counseling in particular is a very time consuming task, and we question whether it is wise for pastors to be heavily involved in it often for a comparatively small number of member couples. As we see it, the first duty of the pastor is to work preventively with the congregation as a whole, doing everything possible to insure that they will not later require marriage counseling. We think he can do much more for the well-being of the marriages in the congregation by devoting his time to preventive services, than by becoming engrossed in the remedial field.°

We are not suggesting that pastors discontinue counseling, but rather that pastors working in close cooperation with a team will discover that a portion of the counselees do not need to be their sole responsibility, but could be the responsibility of a caring team. Pastors often feel compelled to keep members in counseling for years because the counselee insists. Also, counseling may continue because the member does not feel better about the marriage, although there is no solution in sight for that particular problem. When a team becomes involved in a situation, a larger group of peers immediately becomes available to hurting persons to minister to them during sessions as well as through other appropriate encounters.

In other cases the team could give oversight to the pastor's helping process. The caring team could provide guidance and accountability for a pastor's counseling. Most pastors would be grateful for support (1) in keeping a counseling process on target, (2) in referring the counselee to other support groups within the church or to resources outside the congregation, or (3) in simply ending the counseling process if this seems appropriate.

The overall purpose of the caring team needs to be stated more explicitly. The team, with a range of gifts and a mandate

---

°Mace, David and Vera. "Clergy Marriage and Family Ministry," *Marriage Enrichment.* Monthly publication of ACME, the Association of Couples for Marriage Enrichment, (Winston-Salem, N.C., July, August, 1982), p. 2.

from the congregation, uses a group experience to struggle with an individual, or a couple, to find a direction in life in a particular crisis situation. It also helps for a variety of persons to struggle together to discern the will of a particular congregation as they interpret God's will for a specific individual or couple.

Now, let us turn to the composition of the team, and the particular role of each member.

We suggest that a caring team should be made up of the pastor (or pastoral team); a representative from the board of elders or deacons (or whatever that group is called); persons-at-large from the congregation; and someone clinically trained in psychology, psychiatry, social work, or other counseling field, if such a person is available.

1. *The pastor or pastoral team.* The pastor needs to be an active team member who believes in utilizing a caring team approach. The degree of involvement and commitment of the pastor is a factor in the success or failure of this model. A pastor often is the first to learn about problems within the congregation and he is contacted by couples seeking marriage or remarriage. The pastor also needs to suggest to those who request help concerning divorce and remarriage, or any other crisis, that he prefers to consult with the team who is expected to act for the congregation within a covenant of confidentiality. Usually pastors are grateful to share the burden of the helping process with caring members of the congregation.

It is rewarding for pastors to watch members of their congregation grow as individuals or as a group. After the team begins to function, additional members of the congregation may get involved in the healing process. This can become a unique experience which they have never before had occasion to be an integral part of, nor to witness.

In one location where there were several pastors, the team chose to function with only one pastor present at each meeting of the team. The situations which involved or concerned that pastor then were presented. This lightened the load for the pastoral team who already were on too many committees.

We underscore again that a caring team needs the commitment of the pastor.

2. *Representative from board of elders (deacons).* We assume that every congregation has some group which gives oversight to the overall spiritual growth of its members. One team member (in addition to the pastor) should be appointed from that group. This is valuable because it provides a continuous link between an official group which gives direction to the congregation as a whole and the caring team which takes on only one aspect of congregational functioning. It also provides a natural channel for accountability of the team's work with the body responsible for the spiritual oversight of the congregation. It keeps these leaders informed about the general direction of the caring team, and helps the team stay within the guidelines set by the congregation.

3.*Persons-at-large from the congregation.* Some experimentation may be required to determine who makes up this group.

It is a good policy to have a number of couples as members of the team. If the mate of the pastor or of the clinically trained person shows any inclination toward being involved, they should be invited. Other persons should be looked at in terms of couple representation when possible.

A single person should also be a member of the team. This could include a young single adult, a middle-aged divorced person, or an older widow or widower. At times their gifts of understanding are deeply needed.

A couple who had each experienced divorce early in life and were now remarried and in good standing were chosen by one congregation. They eagerly accepted this assignment as if it had been made to order for them and commented that, for once, even their past marital breakup proved to be an asset in the church.

4. *The clinically trained person.* We believe it is very helpful to have a professional counselor or therapist as a member of the team. The key role which this person plays is to facilitate the healing process. This does not mean that the counselor is in charge of the team's operation, but rather knows enough about a healing process to help the team achieve its goals. At times, skills in group

work are required to keep the team from getting bogged down, or worse yet, engaging in activities harmful to an individual or couple. Even well-meaning church members may inadvertently do more harm than good. This may be prevented if the process is carried on under the guidance of a skilled person.

When a clinically trained person is on the team, then each member is freed to exercise his or her unique gifts and insights, knowing someone in the group is giving oversight to the process, and will call attention to activities that may hinder attainment of the healing goals.

Most clinical counselors and therapists are trained to facilitate the healing process in the midst of varied conditions. Some may need help to see how this skill can be utilized by a team. The trained person should understand the unique dynamics of this service, as well as the unique contribution of each team member, and then aid the team to guide the process of helping the person in need in the most appropriate way.

The trained person may choose to see the individual or couple alone for a separate session, or series of sessions, to do some in-depth counseling, and then return the task to the team as soon as possible. If this should require a lengthy process, it may be best to refer the counselee to a competent counselor who is not a member of the team.

What about the congregation that does not have the services of a clinical counselor available to a team? This problem is often not as prevalent as it once was because Christians are entering the counseling field in increased numbers. At times, we believe it could be valid to go outside the congregation to obtain this assistance from a Christian counselor. There are some trained persons who would consider this a voluntary service which provides public exposure for their practice or agency. It would also be appropriate to purchase these services. This might prove to be a better use of a "benevolent fund" than to offer financial assistance to members to find help.

Congregations who do not have a trained counselor in their membership could encourage or support a qualified person to secure further education in social work, clinical psychology, or counseling and guidance. These are usually two-year graduate programs which include a major segment of supervised clinical experience. A middle-aged person who is ready for a vocational transition might be encouraged to return to school for this training. It is possible that persons who know that their gifts could be utilized in the congregation would be inspired to pay the price of such training.

In many congregations the selection of team members is not difficult. It is already known who the persons are who have demonstrated deep concern for family life in the congregation and have tried to get responses. Compassionate persons naturally should be included on the team.

The availability of time is a key factor in team membership. One congregation put service on the team on such a high priority that the members were asked to withdraw from other official congregational involvement so that they might give this assignment first priority. We have found that careful scheduling of team meetings is essential to keep the number of meetings to a minimum. Individuals or couples to be seen by a team need to be willing to adjust their schedule to the team's meeting times.

Committed persons must be available to make the work of the team effective. If this vision is lost by a team member, then it is advisable to replace that team member with someone ready for the challenge.

The following qualifications for team membership were explicitly defined by a congregation who adopted the team approach:

1. The person must be a member of this congregation, in good standing and in agreement with the congregation's policy on divorce and remarriage.

2. The person must evidence genuine compassion for those who are hurting and be able to demonstrate it by balancing care for hurting people with clarity about appropriate courses of action in a given situation.

3. The person must be knowledgeable in the Word of God

and be able to apply the principles of Scripture to specific situations which may arise.

4. The person must be able to maintain confidentiality in all matters discussed on the team and with individuals and couples in work related functions.

5. The person must be willing to intercede in prayer regularly on behalf of the families and couples of the church.

It is difficult to describe the personal reward that comes with membership on the caring team. It is exhilarating to see the congregation dotted with persons who were helped, especially when it is evident that certain couples would now be divorced if the team had not intervened at the time of crisis. Others might have ignored the remarriage regulations and fled, finding it too painful to return to that church later. To watch these persons become faithful church attenders and participants is rewarding.

After months or, in some cases, years of struggle with a particular remarriage situation, team members have shared many joyous experiences including attendance at the wedding. Later, when a pregnancy occurred and a child was born, the couple searched for team members on their first Sunday back to show a new baby in their arms. There is a distinct nonverbal statement something like this, "See, here is our precious infant. If you had not stood by us and supported us at that crucial time, it would not have been this way."

After a few experiences like these, team members seem to be able to give a high priority to team membership. This type of rewarding experience is common to a counselor's office, but rarely is it experienced by members in the congregation. An invitation to membership on a caring team is an invitation to be involved in a healing process that affirms an individual's Christian calling. It also affirms the calling of the congregation to be a healing instrument for God's people.

9

Redemptive Caring in the Remarriage Process

Dealing with divorce and remarriage calls for a carefully guided process by a caring group. The first illustration below is an experience of a congregation which had no effective means to deal with a difficult situation. The second illustrates a guided redemptive process.

Ten years had passed since Dick's wife took an overdose and died. She had suffered for years from depression, but little was known about the marital situation. During these years Dick raised his three teenage sons in an admirable fashion. The four attended services regularly for many years.

Dick became a pathetic single adult in the congregation. Frequently he stopped at the pastor's office for chats. These visits were for social and diversionary purposes rather than for specific direction or counseling. Generally, people pitied Dick since he handled his single status rather poorly. He was unable to put into words the things that bothered him. People tended to be friendly, but relationships were superficial. Dick appeared to keep himself from any deep social involvements. He was a hurting widower who spent his time on the fringes of congregational life.

The congregation provided no services to meet Dick's needs. Individuals tried to reach him, but his aloofness made this nonproductive. The pastor's attempts were usually slipped into superficial conversation. After a while the pastor resorted to a more appropriate process. He spent time with Dick in Bible study and prayer. The spiritual counseling was helpful in that it taught Dick to have a regular devotional life of his own.

Another congregation sponsored a single adult program. Dick joined this group. Instead of using the program to become comfortable about being single, he spent his time looking for loners like himself. Soon he met Ann, a middle-aged divorcée who had managed her years of singleness as poorly as he. As a result, two desperately lonely people instantly clung to each other. They called it love, romance, and courtship.

Ann contacted her pastor to get some perspective on this process. Events happened too fast for her. The pastor was empathetic and listened carefully. Then he listed several issues that she needed to explore and attempted to help her carefully examine a number of possible pitfalls.

Ann had been a divorcée for more than 15 years. Her four children were grown and married. She had not understood why her husband had a series of affairs, nor did she have any notion as to what she did, or failed to do, to make him finally divorce her. Ann's pastor could do little to help her, since he had personally never met her husband. However, he was able to show that he cared about her.

After several counseling sessions Ann decided to cool the courtship process. In this Ann had her pastor's support, although neither of them had concrete reasons for this action. It just did not feel right.

When Dick was informed about Ann's reluctance to proceed, he immediately contacted his pastor to secure his help to have Ann change her mind. Dick felt strongly that it was God's will that they should get married and that he needed to get this message through to Ann's pastor and to Ann.

When Dick's pastor told Ann about Dick's feelings, she was unable to resist his strong proposal. She was approaching her fiftieth year and had known enough loneliness. Her children had often told her, "Oh, Mom, why don't you forget Dad and get married. You can start over again." So why not? She was not sure where God's will fit into this whole scene, but at least Dick and his pastor did. Maybe that was enough. Since she was told that God was already directing it so obviously now, God would surely direct this marital process.

Once Ann yielded to the pressure, wedding plans were quickly made by Dick and his pastor. A short time later Ann left her apartment and moved into Dick's large comfortable home. She was married to a man she had met only two months earlier and hardly knew.

It took only a few months after the marriage for Ann to wake up to one horrible fact. Dick had an exact ideal of what a wife ought to be like. This was the mold that he had created for his first wife, and now it was to fit her also. Nothing was negotiable. Ann knew at once why Dick's first wife had overdosed. This was not an option for her. First, she tried to reason with Dick and negotiate her needs, but he had no desire to do that. Then she demanded that they seek help, which he refused. The deadlock was final, so she filed for divorce and legally resumed her former name.

Ann severed her ties with the pastor and the congregation, completely confused as to how such a nightmare could have happened in the name of Christianity.

A correct process could possibly have brought about healing. Proper negotiating by caring persons at the right time could have been what Dick and Ann really needed to prevent disaster.

The faulty pieces in this entire process can be discerned. Neither of these persons had learned from their first marriages. Yet they could and should have understood what went wrong before they remarried. There should be a way to learn. Dick's single state was a burden to the congregation and to the pastor. There should have been a system, worked out ahead of time, which would have guided a decision-making process. The most destructive factor was the lack of a process which could have opened up the real issues that each of these persons should have spread out together, before a caring, praying group. A caring team could have guided them through a healthy compromise or resolution before any wedding commitment was made.

Each of these two pastors and congregations had a need for a previously worked through healing system so that it could be called upon to intervene. Hopefully, a congregation that cares about marriages, and especially about divorces and those persons seeking remarriage, will create a method for responding to people like Dick and Ann. All divorce and remarriage situations are complicated. Extreme caution and care needs to be exercised by pastors, congregations and caring teams. Therefore, it is important to establish a clearly defined process before divorce and remarriage situations are encountered. The caring team is one model created to serve this need. This model has been tested in one congregation for ten years and more recently in a number of others.

The next example shows how the caring team was used in a difficult remarriage situation. The congregation worked through the issues, in advance, so that an immediate spiritually enlightened response was possible.

Ellen fearfully approached the pastor of her congregation about her desire to accept a marriage proposal from Harold, a divorcé. Ellen had grown up in the congregation, but was uncertain where the congregation stood regarding divorce and remarriage. In no way did she want to jeopardize her standing in the congregation.

Ellen was especially concerned about her four married children and several grandchildren who considered this congregation as their spiritual home. She did not want her remarriage to cause major distress for anyone concerned.

On the other side was another factor. Harold, with three teenage children, happened on the scene and he was absolutely sincere in his intentions for both of them. Since Harold was from another congregation of the same denomination, he knew that he was creating a dilemma for Ellen. He also was willing to drop out of her life if this was disturbing her conscience or was a transgression of her congregation's practice.

Since her husband's death several years ago, Ellen lived by herself in acute loneliness. Nothing about her nature was built for singleness. She loved to care for someone. She had enjoyed cooking, cleaning, and caring for the house for her husband, and he showed appreciation for her work. Now all the desire to do this, or anything else, vanished. The road ahead looked dismal until Harold came along. He, like her first husband, John, needed someone to organize and manage even the small affairs of his life. And she loved to do this.

Ellen did not want her spiritual commitment to Christ and to the local congregation to be adversely affected. However, at the same time she felt God was calling her to the new marriage. Ellen's questions to her pastor were: "Should I or should I not accept the proposal? What is the position of the congregation? What is your opinion?"

Fortunately, Ellen's pastor could respond immediately to her in an affirming redemptive way, without making a decision. Her congregation had appointed a caring team. The pastor explained to Ellen that there was a procedure worked out which would involve her, and also Harold if he agreed, in a marriage preparation process. The question of marriage depended on their willingness to go along with this team on a journey that would insure as healthy and wholesome a marriage as possible. If they were open to counseling with the caring team, and if the team recommended that they proceed, he would marry them. The congregation, as a whole, would accept the decision if processed in this way.

Ellen's immediate response was, "That sounds good! I'm sure that Harold will also cooperate. I believe he will like it, especially because he is concerned that his former marriage and divorce may eventually bother me. We need to talk to someone about this. We need to talk about our former marriages. There may be things we have not really dealt with. We are also concerned about our children. My children know that we believe in the permanency of marriage. Am I disobeying my own teaching? With all of my past assumptions about the wrongness of remarriage, I guess I need help to come to peace spiritually before I am ready to go ahead."

The pastor called the chairperson of the team while Ellen was still in the office. He needed to check out the best strategy to begin the process. They concurred that it would be best to begin with a meeting of Ellen and the team, since she was a member of the congregation. At the beginning, the team and Ellen needed to sort out the issues without involving Harold. Since he was a member of another congregation, the team also had to discuss the complications that might arise in involving Harold's pastor and that body of believers before Harold should be invited into the process.

The first meeting of the team with Ellen was a beautiful worship experience. The pastor led in prayer, asking God to guide everyone in this venture. He asked that all of the discussion and all of the decisions be made with the awareness that they were acting in Christ's stead as they were being a congregation who seeks to heal the wounds of the couple involved.

Ellen's first concern was how one could be certain that marriage to a divorced person was within God's will. The team took turns in sharing their views. They told her that they believed that the work of the team was the work of their congregation, and thus the work of Christ on earth at this location. They emphasized that everything would be done prayerfully. In no way did this change the plan of God — that marriages are lifelong commitments. However, the team was aware that sin did exist in this world and that sin had been committed in this particular divorce. It was the ultimate goal of the congregation to heal the brokenhearted, to care for those who fall, and to show the way to restoration and wholeness. The caring team would carefully discern many of the spiritual, interpersonal, and emotional issues involved and then plan a course of action. The final outcome would reflect God's intent because the team was acting in his love. The decision about marriage would be made by everyone present, acting on behalf of the congregation, and in line with its understandings, and thus God's will would also be reflected.

Ellen had already talked to her children who supported her completely. Since they knew that the team existed and were acquainted with the members, they were confident that all would be done with care and discretion. Ellen's family assured her that if the outcome of this process were remarriage, then they would accept Harold as their stepfather and support them both in every way possible. Her family offered to meet with the team if this would be of value. But since they knew of other cases which the team had handled and they were completely confident about the outcome, they could see no reason to have such a session. They were grateful that their mother had this resource to help her work through this problem because they felt that they were too closely related to be objective.

After Ellen explained the process of her congregation to Harold, he was surprised that such a system existed within his own denomination. Although he was completely ready to go along with this process, he was also totally unsure about the reaction of his pastor or his congregation. He asked if, somehow, he might be spared the agony of having to cope with his own congregation.

The team decided that Ellen's pastor and the chairperson would meet with Harold's pastor to see if his congregation would be ready to be involved in the reconciliation process. The main reason for involving Harold's congregation was to continue the entire process of reconciliation that would engulf members of another congregation who also might need healing. If they could be engaged, then the redeeming work of Christ would spread even further. It also would ensure Harold that he could turn to his own community of faith, later on, if he needed them. Since the team was so enthused about the healing process, they hoped to pass this method on to every congregation possible.

The meeting with Ellen continued with suggestions of areas of concern that still needed exploration. A touchy issue arose immediately. Ellen was formerly married to John, a prominent congregational leader who was highly esteemed. John had served a term on the board of elders and was highly respected by the people who knew him, whereas Harold's extreme marital problems that existed for years had left him in a questionable position in the congregation. Harold's divorce, although necessary for his emotional survival, was completely misunderstood. Therefore he deliberately remained on the fringes of the congregation. The question the team asked Ellen was simply, "Have you thought about this and, if so, how will you cope with this if you marry?"

Ellen had given a great deal of thought to this and answered with a lot of conviction. She and Harold had spent long hours talking about their quite different reactions to the congregation. For Ellen, the congregation was a caring community who rallied by her side at every need, especially during the worst of calamities. Harold had a lot of bruises. His wish was that he might experience the ministering, healing congregation as she had. The first step was for the caring team to prove to Harold that they cared about him and knew what to do in this situation.

Another concern was that it appeared that the recent death of Ellen's husband might make Harold's schedule for remarriage out of keeping with hers. He, after all, had been separated for a long, long time. The team asked Ellen if she could accept their time schedule and convey the team's concern to Harold. Ellen agreed to tell Harold and expressed gratitude that the timing was left to someone else's judgment rather than hers. She replied, "The whole courtship with Harold appears so right that I may just be blinded. I'm glad you are here to guide me."

The meeting with Harold's pastor proved to be difficult. At first, he brought up theological issues. In his mind, he could not accept the rightness of any Christian's remarriage following divorce. The pastor also was familiar with Harold's divorce and had not forgotten the pain experienced by the congregation. The team needed to refocus the issues, from an ideal biblical answer to a more practical redemptive response. It also took a lot of effort to explain the procedure of the team. Harold's pastor became intrigued, as he began to realize that this really was a positive step which a courageous congregation had taken. He asked whether it would be appropriate to have Harold transfer membership immediately and thus have the whole issue settled for his congregation since they were not prepared to deal with the issue at this time.

The question of Harold's first wife also came up in this conversation. The pastor explained that she left the congregation early in the marital breakup process. He was not sure where she now lived. All he knew was that she had remarried and probably would not cooperate in any way at this time. It was agreed that it would be risky to attempt to involve her. However, greater healing might result for both of them if this were possible.

At the next meeting with Harold and Ellen, the team suggested that Harold transfer his membership to Ellen's congregation. This was necessary to avoid a major eruption in Harold's home congregation. The team assured Harold that his pastor appeared receptive to the entire working procedure and felt a need to help his congregation rethink its position on divorce and remarriage. However, to do this when it was forced upon them by a request for remarriage would be poor timing. Such a study could focus primarily on his specific remarriage which would affect the thinking of the congregation. Harold accepted the suggestion of transfer.

Since they felt the need to reflect on as many issues as possible, the team met with Harold and Ellen for several months. Harold and Ellen found the prayerful support of the team meaningful. They always arrived at each session eager to explore the issues facing them.

The date for the wedding was finally set and the wedding was conducted according to a combined plan worked through with the couple and the caring team.

A week prior to the wedding, as Harold was accepted into membership, a delegate from the team made an explanation to the congregation.

It was necessary to say that this was a remarriage for Harold even though most members of the congregation already knew that. It also was important to mention that the team had carefully worked with Harold's former pastor and with Harold's and Ellen's children.

The wedding was a small private celebration with immediate family members. Assisted by the team and the couple, Ellen's pastor wrote the wedding ceremony. (See Appendix C.) This was a wedding which involved remarriage for both partners.

Several years have now passed and Harold and Ellen have blended into the congregation. When a team member met them after a recent church service and asked them whether they felt the congregation had any problem accepting them, they said that they had not experienced any difficulty. People actually continue to go out of their way to be extra gracious to them. Harold and Ellen feel that this response comes from a need to be extra loving since people know that they experienced enough pain earlier. Individuals seem to be trying to make it up to them with special caring now.

10

The Caring Core:
A Local Church Experiment

When a seed is planted in rich soil, at the right time under good conditions and properly watered, it will sprout and grow into a large plant. Such an event is a pleasure to watch. This is exactly how we felt as we watched a local congregation in southeastern Pennsylvania accept the kernel of truth about the creation of a caring team. It took only seven months from the time they first heard of the idea until it was a major ministry of the congregation, alive and growing.

We shall trace the events in detail to encourage other congregations to use the same seed and nurture it.

(It is important to keep in mind that every congregation is different. Each must work in its own way. Each congregation's team will be different, but it will fill the unique needs at that location. Smaller congregations will need to find variations appropriate to their size. Sometimes a cluster of congregations may decide to form a single team.)

In many ways this large congregation with several hundred members is quite conventional. It is an independent, unaffiliated evangelical congregation. The message they proclaim is clear and powerful. They ask every member to have a "born-again" experience to bring them into a right relationship with God. Members are encouraged to speak about their faith with whomever they can.

The congregation believes in the centrality of the Bible as the inspired Word of God and that it needs to be read prayerfully as a source of guidance for faith and practice. The central theme of their belief is Jesus Christ, his sacrificial death, his resurrection, ascension, and his awaited return. Theologically, they are solidly evangelical.

Geographically, the congregation is situated on the boundary of the sprawling Philadelphia urban poor and the suburban mainline of the middle and wealthy upper class. The congregation is made up largely of middle-class persons.

Any evangelistic appeal by the congregation brings with it the response of those in the immediate community as well as a share of the marital and social problems prevalent in the adjoining city.

In speaking with members, we received the impression that they are quite clear about the faith they profess and believe. However, they are conscious of their Christian mandate to respond to the social needs around them. When they read their Bibles and ponder the passage "When I was hungry you gave me food," they know firsthand who Jesus was talking about. (See Matthew 25:35-40.) Our second impression was that their members had difficulty knowing how to respond to these needs.

What makes them most unconventional is the man they selected as their pastor. The pastor is a graduate of a Bible college, has attended seminary, and holds a doctorate in social work. He initially accepted the pastorate of this congregation only on a temporary basis because he really wanted to devote himself to the profession for which he was trained. This pastor and the congregation have developed an increasingly deepened commitment to one another and he is presently a much loved permanent pastor.

It was the pastor's social consciousness that gave him the vision to help this congregation create a community services outreach as a ministry of the congregation. Their social welfare agency provides highly skilled services to individuals, married couples, and families through trained and committed Christian therapists. In addition, the agency operates child care and nursery facilities in the main church building. The program also provides a senior citizens' ministry, voluntary emergency services, and family life education. As one would expect, the pastor personally serves as the director of the center and supervises many of the staff members and services.

Although these services were effective to clients and drew congregational members as volunteers, they did not become an integral part of the congregation as had been expected. The services did not enable the body of believers to become part of the caring process personally. Those in need of help still were referred outside of the congregation to the services provided next door. Although the congregation initiated the ministry and gave the services effectively, it still provided no vehicle for them, as a body of believers, to directly care for their own needy persons.

Then a fateful event occurred. A couple in the congregation had a marital difficulty which became known to the congregation. The couple could easily have been referred next door where professional intervention was readily available. However, the congregation stood by helplessly as they were told something like this: "Cover this matter with silence. This is not a time for gossip nor well-intentioned criticism. Instead we must pray intelligently and continuously on their behalf. Forgive the couple and encourage and help them as they build their relationship back together. Pray for other couples in our congregation who need God's healing in their marriages. Also pray that our board and others will be able to minister compassionately to those in our congregation where needs such as this are evident. God is at work in our congregation. We have asked him to break us and make us like Christ—that we may serve him."

The pastor came to us and asked what our response would be in a situation like this. When he heard about our model for congregational conciliation with broken individuals and marriages, he understood the unique dynamics of this entire concept. After clearing the idea in general terms with the the board of deacons, the pastor made an urgent appeal to the congregation. He based his message on the pertinent Scriptural passages, Galatians 5:25—

6:2 (KJV): "If we live in the Spirit, let us also walk in the Spirit. Let us not be desirous of vain glory, provoking one another, envying one another. Brethren, if a man be overtaken in a fault, ye which are spiritual, restore such an one in the spirit of meekness; considering thyself, lest thou also be tempted. Bear ye one another's burdens, and so fulfil the law of Christ."

The pastor then proceeded to tell the congregation that this Scripture had a direct bearing on all of them at this time.

"We need to function as the body of Christ, as a community of believers in him. We have a responsibility to care—to mutually care for one another. Every epistle in the New Testament emphasizes the responsibility we have for one another, to care." To support this statement he read 1 Corinthians 12:25-27 (KJV): "That there should be no schism in the body; but that the members should have the same care one for another. And whether one member suffers, all the members suffer with it; or one member be honoured, all the members rejoice with it. Now ye are the body of Christ, and members in particular."

With no apology the pastor underscored the idea that persons in their congregation are members of one another as clearly stated. He asked if they, indeed, do suffer with those who suffer. He did not wait for an answer when he said, "That does not seem to be the state of affairs in the Christian church today."

He continued, "Have you ever come into the congregation, and as you are sitting there another member of the congregation comes in and you know that person is hurting? You know that there is a division in the home, or that there is another problem. Perhaps a husband and wife are having trouble between themselves that they don't know how to handle. And neither do you! You sit there and think, 'I see that. I see it happening.' You pray, perhaps, but you do not have the means, the vehicle, to reach out and care for that person."

How could anyone there not have understood what he meant? The vivid awareness of the troubled couple was still fresh in their memories. All knew they did nothing because there was nothing they could do.

The pastor continued, "Our helplessness has left us out in the cold. So we attend church and then we go our ways. There is little if any sense of mutual care."

He told the congregation that they were in many respects a warm, caring, and affectionate people. He was grateful for their expression of this after the formal service when they often clustered around each other to visit, but that was not what he meant.

"You know that this caring needs to extend beyond ourselves, beyond those who are mutually caring for each other, to those who for one reason or another can't care because they are hurting too much. We need to reach out and embrace them, too. We need to bring them into the care and protection of the body of Christ so that healing can occur. If there is sin involved, it must be dealt with, so that restoration and healing can take place. And, beloved, that is a demonstration of redemption. That is what God wants to do in the first place for people who are outside of Christ."

Hurting persons can't participate in the body of faith by themselves, so someone has to reach out and bring them in and be the reconciling message of the gospel of Jesus Christ to them.

The congregation knew this Scripture passage well. They knew they had not heeded it. They knew what the problem was, but they did not know how to respond effectively.

To add to his argument the pastor shared a paragraph from a book he had been reading:°

> An alarming reason for the failure of evangelical marriages is the church's silence concerning its ancient function for caring for its marriages. In turn, couples with marriage problems have turned everywhere but to the church to seek help. The time has come for the church to aggressively return to its God-given role of disciplining the marriages of its members."

If this was not enough, he then turned to a section in the church's own constitution:

°Gerald L. Dahl, *Why Christian Marriages Are Breaking Up* (Nashville: Thomas Nelson, 1979), p. 131.

Each member should cherish and cultivate love for all other members of the church, visit and sympathize with them in affliction, pray for and with them, administer relief to those who are in need, tenderly regard their reputation, affectionately and privately admonish them for faults and inproprieties, and strive by all proper measures to promote their spiritual benefit and prosperity.

He said, "That's in our constitution, and I am so glad its there, because I believe with all my heart that's what we as a people of God ought to be doing as part of our ministry in the body of Christ. That is even in the section that has to do with the expulsion of a member of the church because of continual misconduct. Our constitution admonishes us that this should not occur until every effort has been exhausted to bring such a person back into fellowship and heal that relationship."

Obviously, everybody must have assumed by now that starting a center with a whole range of services for hurting humanity should be sufficient. Not one congregation in a thousand had done this. So what more could he be asking of them?

The pastor continued, "I'm coming to the conclusion that the center for this ministry is inadequate. It is inadequate."

After this he proposed that the congregation establish a caring team to carry out the mandate of the Bible and the church constitution to promote redemption and healing among individuals, marriages, and families within the congregation.

He then presented the caring team model as described in earlier chapters and reviewed the specific proposals he was now making to the board of deacons.

Later, the pastor reminded the congregation of a strange policy which they had taken in regards to divorce and remarriage.

"We will accept remarried people into the fellowship of our congregation, but it is also a matter of policy that we will not perform the wedding ceremony. If remarriage is an appropriate course of action for some people, then perhaps as a congregation, we ought to consider whether marrying these people may also be an appropriate course of action.

"The policy is inconsistent and we don't have any vehicle to deal with couples like this. Our rationale for not marrying them may have less to do with whether it's right or wrong than with protecting the reputation of our church from attack from the outside. 'Why are you remarrying these people?' But if we had a procedure for counseling with couples who are seeking our help, it might make a large difference in how we handle the problem of remarriage in our church.

"If we are a congregation of people who are genuinely concerned about the specific needs of a hurting couple in the congregation, if we are willing to meet with that couple and teach them to grow, it's a misuse of the center next door for us to turn that couple over to one person to deal with the issue. Here is a whole group of a couple hundred people caring and carrying the burden for a couple and all of a sudden it wants a person ouside the congregation to deal with them. We are talking about a body of believers who, in Jesus Christ, have a different quality to give to the couple than the center. What the center has to give is important, but we can never let it be the only thing that we give to our couples. There needs to be shepherding, spiritual undergirding for those in our congregation who need help.

"We want to develop a caring sensitive way in which we can help couples and families in our congregation when they struggle." To accomplish this the pastor proposed that a caring team be established within the congregation.

"There are times when you, as well as I, may need the services of this group. I can't imagine any greater comfort, when a couple feels alone, confused, and lost about the direction to go than to be able to come to a team of the church and say, 'Will you pray with us, bear with us, struggle with us, through this problem we face?' Wouldn't it be great for a team to garner sensitively the strength of the entire congregation and bring to bear prayer and stand with that couple until they find a way through their trouble? I'm convinced that can begin to happen. We can see a major turnaround in this congregation in terms of helping Christian couples avoid breaking up.

"I feel sad as I look over our congregation. There are a number of people in our congregation whose marriages right now are hurting, some who are in second marriages, and others who have been separated from the first marriage and are in limbo. Up to this time, where has the help come from? I suggest that a special team be formed to address a specific issue that the body of Christ ought to be deeply involved in as a demonstration of the love of Christ and what redemption is all about."

Then the pastor ended the service in the most unusual way. In their services it is customary to have an altar call, or at least to provide an occasion to rededicate themselves to the new enlightenment of the message. Instead, every person present was asked to write on a piece of paper the names of the three persons in their congregation whom they considered to be the most compassionate—"The three people you would feel most comfortable going to if your marriage were in trouble." He then told them that they were nominating three persons for the caring team.

"I trust you will be really praying. I believe God can use this congregation in specific practical ways, just like this, to be a demonstration of his love in this area of the world. And the Lord knows the church is crying for this kind of healing."

The first response he received following the service was the suggestion that the name of the team be changed to "The Caring Core." To that member, such a name better defined the purpose of the team. "At the core of this church there should be a group who are caring in special ways for some hurting individuals, couples, or families," the member said. (That name was adopted later.)

The results of the nomination of caring persons were remarkable. A total of seventy different names were suggested! Of this number twelve persons were nominated more than ten times.

The pastor then wrote a memo to the board of deacons specifically outlining his proposal for the caring team and received a resounding affirmative vote. With the nominations in hand they selected a group of eleven persons.

The fact that the team is as large as this is certainly different from what we had seen in other congregations. Later reports indicate that this congregation finds this size manageable.

Another decision that was made by this congregation is also unique. The Caring Core planned to meet every Sunday morning during the Sunday school hour. Every person contacted was asked to make this group's task a major priority in their work in the congregation, so it meant that they had to resign their positions if they were teaching in the Sunday school. They also had to leave the group that they belonged to for that study hour and devote their allegiance to this new group.

The Caring Core also decided that the meeting time would be spent together, not only to deal with other people, but also for their own edification. They would search the Scripture for a clearer understanding of the theological issues involved in divorce and remarriage and the whole concept of the church as it responds to the social and interpersonal needs of people.

When we questioned a team member whether this was not too big a task to take on, we received a negative answer. She loved being part of a group that was grappling with such vital matters and then had the authority and means to act. This involvement was very exciting for her.

We visited the congregation seven months later to assess the early results of The Caring Core in action.

It was immediately obvious to us that we were observing an unusual pastor and an unusual congregation. Where but in that congregation could one find a person committed to Christ and dedicated to the ministry with the skill to proclaim the gospel message clearly, who also held the highest degree in social work? He was a skillful therapist and had recently been elected as an approved supervisor with the American Association for Marriage and Family Therapy. Under his guidance, it was no wonder that the team had so quickly consolidated into an effective working arm of the congregation.

The group had now been organized with the full sanction of the congregation and board of deacons. They were meeting every Sunday morning. Several crucial, complicated individual, marital, and family situations called for immediate response. So now that they were in action an assessment seemed in order.

This is the pastor's summary of the work of the team. "For our congregation, I see the work of The Caring Core as a model of what Christian community and responsibility is all about.

"It seems to me, theologically, our brand of Christianity in the twentieth century has concentrated too much on individualism. One's relationship to the Lord has primarily become an individual matter. That leaves out much of the emphasis on community: the responsibility for one another, mutual caring, strengthening a person's sense that he is not alone in his struggles. All those things seem not to be in the present expression of Christianity that comes out of many independent churches. The very ideal of independence suggests, 'We'll do it ourselves.' Each person gets the idea that they must do it alone. When people get into trouble, particularly over something that is sinful or shameful, the first reaction is to go and hide. If they want to do anything different, they can't. There is no formal way to seek counsel within the congregation. I see this as a major need which The Caring Core can help satisfy.

"We do not have to alienate each other by our individualism. We see this team as a way back from individualism to a church functioning as a community, especially at times when people experience marital or family crises.

"We have on our agenda to recommend policy on who may be married in our church, and how to shepherd people into the congregation. The Caring Core can address those types of issues.

"We meet every week. We have agreed that we are not counselors. We are caring persons. If there is a need for professional counseling, we have other resources. We make referrals and stay in touch with the counseling process."

Although this congregation accepted the basic premise of our caring team model, they adapted it to their congregation. Thus the group now has dynamics which are entirely their own.

Their team is willing to take on every alienation problem—anyone who is involved in any sin and is out of fellowship with the Lord and the congregation. The team deals with all separation from the body of Christ. They are doing this because it is a real need in this congregation. It is a congregation which does not have an emphasis on being a family of God. They need help in becoming such a caring community. They also have a qualified pastor to guide this process.

The size and makeup of the team are unique. There was an attempt to make it as diverse as possible. It includes a retired widow, a young single man, a young couple, a middle-aged couple, an older couple, and a couple in which both members are divorced and remarried. This group also serves as the means whereby the congregation can address the entire policy issue on divorce and remarriage in the congregation.

One distinctive task this group assumed was the use of their benevolent fund when it was appropriate. The group works with the people who are helped financially by the congregation. The Caring Core assumes responspibility for helping the recipients use the money appropriately, as well as encouraging them not to remain dependent, if at all possible. This method differs from that of most congregations who offer financial assistance to needy persons with little guidance about the use of the funds.

The enormity of the task which this group is assuming could create a problem. They are concerned about the overload factor, but they are ready to have other support groups formed to take over on a particular need. They see coordination of the healing process as the major key for offering help. Therefore they have confined their meetings as a group to Sunday mornings. Anything done by individuals on this team during the week is entirely voluntary and not required of them. It is their belief that if the right direction is given, God will provide the healing. Enthusiasm runs so high at this time that no one thinks too much is expected of team members. The gratifying results they have seen so far seem to make it all worthwhile.

This illustration shows how the caring team concept was shaped to fit one particular congregation. Because of the problems the congregation had faced recently, they could easily claim ownership and utilize the model. It is no wonder that the idea sprouted quickly, grew rapidly, and bore fruit in due season.

11

A Design
for Congregational Caring

In an era when the material needs of congregational members have been replaced largely by emotional, relational, and interpersonal needs, how best can a congregation respond? All the resources—the tithe of members' gifts, skills, and potential—need to be gathered and distributed generously to persons in need.

It is not as easy as taking an offering and dividing the proceeds to those in need. The best of the healing skills and gifts from within the congregation are pooled and a systematic means is created to utilize this healing potential skillfully and effectively wherever need arises. Stewardship of more than financial gifts is required; stewardship of congregational caring is also important.

The solution we propose is that the healing potential be gathered together in a caring group that functions according to good healing principles. The caring team follows a carefully and prayerfully guided process to dispense healing to the broken and hurting members of a congregation.

To carry out this design most effectively, certain guidelines need to be followed.

1. There must be an awareness of God's desire for wholeness.

The congregation exists to act in God's stead to bring wholeness to all persons within its reach. We recognize God's desire for wholeness for all.

In the beginning it was not so. If God could have kept it that way, he would have. God desires that the dissensions between himself and humankind be mended. To close this gap God came in Christ that all may be saved (made whole). Those who believe in Jesus and accept him as their Savior and Lord are spiritually restored in their relationship to God. He has also provided the Holy Spirit who empowers each believer to live in loving obedience. However, due to the fallen state of humanity, brokenness still exists in many other areas of life. This calls for special caring by the congregation.

The primary function of the church is to proclaim the message of salvation, inviting all persons into this new union with God. The church is also expected to reach out in love to help persons experience the love of God in daily living. Where brokenness occurs, in whatever form, it is the church's obligation to respond however it can to undo the fallen state of humanity. This charge is given to the church in general and to each congregation in particular.

Each member is to express love, acceptance and forgiveness. Where needs call for special help, a caring team can be created to help in carrying out this task in a congregation that yearns for wholeness among persons and between individuals and God.

2. A congregation must have a passionate concern for broken lives.

This model functions best in a congregation which cares for all its members and for all persons it touches. The more loving the congregation is, the more effective will be the team's response and functioning. It is best if it is known both within the congregation, as well as in the surrounding community, that the people who worship at a location care for people to the extent that where there is hurt, they pray, yearn for wholeness, and sacrifice for broken lives to be healed.

When the caring team functions in this setting, it will be an integral part of the congregation's total position and not something that is artificially tacked on. It also means that team members will not need to spend a lot of time justifying their work. It will be mutually understood that the team's effort is a style of caring that is a specialized expression of what members are doing, even if parts are borrowed from secular counseling, psychology, and therapy.

3. Team members must be personally committed to caring.

There is no question that membership on the team is a time and energy-consuming assignment. However, members must be committed enough to contribute their efforts ungrudgingly. Since the entire task of the team is to deal with personal and interpersonal failure, the work can be discouraging. This is the price that needs to be paid for loving those who need an extra dose of love. Members selected must be those who have the gift of compassion and who desire to exercise this gift. It is best if they receive much personal satisfaction from spontaneously caring for people in need.

The members of the team can carry out their task only if it flows naturally from their inner beings, rather than from a reluctant sense of obligation.

4. The congregation must support the team graciously.

For the team to function, it must have the absolute loyalty of the congregation. This means the congregation must trust a small group of its members to function with a covenant of confidentiality. They must trust that some decisions in applying the faith understandings of the congregation need to be made without congregational vote.

Every member of the congregation has the right to ask questions of team members, and is entitled to an honest answer, unless it involves confidential material. Members of the congregation are also invited to express their opinions. However, they must then be willing to allow the team to act in their stead.

For a caring team to function best, the congregation must trust the healing process and the caring team even though they may not fully understand or fully know what is happening.

5. The team is responsible to operate confidentially.

This means that the team has the right to discuss the personal lives and the marital welfare of any member of the congregation without that person's knowledge, or without accountability to that individual or to other persons. For the team to function, it must survey the needy areas in the congregation and explore troubled lives and decide what healing resources are most appropriate for a particular need. If the team decides to intervene it must have the right to offer the course of action it feels is best. A congregation should give the team the freedom it needs to act effectively.

6. The team is expected to give counsel.

A group of people acting as the body of Christ must have expectations of one another. The giving and receiving of counsel, the binding and loosing,° and forgiveness occur when the Spirit is present in Christ's church. It is in keeping with God's will that it be acceptable to a congregation that some decisions are made by a group that represents them. After all, Christ himself has said that where two or three are gathered in his name, he would be with them (Matthew 18:20). The individual receiving counsel must know that this is the will of the congregation and thus part of God's will also.

In actual practice this means that members of the team have the responsibility to approach erring members and invite them to meet with the team in an effort to find healing. The motive of the team is not to chastise, nor to identify the person's error. Rather, it is to point the way to healing. The team assumes the task of leading the way to spiritual and emotional health.

7. The caring team could be expected to act on matters involving church membership.

Membership in the congregation is not merely a matter of in-

°See *A Third Way* by Paul M. Lederach (Scottdale: Herald Press, 1980), pp. 44-48, for more on "binding and loosing."

dividual rights. It involves a commitment to a fellowship of believers. The team could be expected to act when this commitment is broken. Suspension or refusal of membership would be recommended only when someone refuses "to give and receive counsel." This should happen only after the efforts of the team have failed to bring restoration of faith and action. (See Matthew 18:15-19.)

The mandate to the caring team could be that they sensitively discern the leading of God with the individual, with the hope of bringing the person to repentance and forgiveness. When this is not possible, it might be necessary to recommend that membership be terminated. The recommendation would be presented to the elders or the group that is responsible for membership matters within the congregation.

8. *The congregation and the team must be willing to identify sin.*

The entire reconciliation process works best in a congregation and with a team that recognizes and calls sin by its name. Skills from behavioral sciences will be used in dealing with each individual, and group skills will be employed to make the team function most effectively. This does not diminish the fact that at the root of many issues is sin. Before a representative group of the congregation can effect wholeness, sin must be named and true forgiveness sought. In the presence of God, the team must recognize when sin is forgiven, and then respond with certainty that God has also forgiven.

9. *The congregation must believe that holiness is God's will.*

There can be no wavering about the fact that God's ultimate will is holiness. This is arrived at by seeking the forgiving love of Christ and then living in his will in grateful submission.

The team's mandate is to strive always to bring about holier lives, regardless of the needs to which they respond.

10. *The counselor must be one who functions beyond professionality.*

The clinically trained member of the team must be sufficiently confident of his or her own skill and be willing to permit the leading of the Spirit to take precedence over professional loyalty. At times, the counselor may be called to support the opinion of a team member who is being led by God, rather than clinical insight. The counselor also needs to seek the Lord's leading in all he or she says and does, and to recognize that spiritual growth can go hand-in-hand with emotional growth.

The more able a counselor is to translate professional expertise into the model described, the more effective the entire team process will be. It is remarkable how helpful a group of persons who traditionally have not been involved in counseling can be when they participate in such a setting. One key to effectiveness is that the counselor translates the resources of the team into a healing process for persons in need.

This model assumes that the clinically trained member is prepared to be innovative and ready to run some risks. However, beyond this it assumes that the clinically trained member is ready to get out of the traditional mode and explore new forms of helping.

11. A pastor who desires team assistance is needed.

For this model to function effectively the pastor must be willing to assume a servant-leader role. Much of what the team is doing once was the private territory of the pastor of a congregation. Many of the decisions which are made by the team ordinarily were made in the office of the pastor.

The greatest test of the servant leader pastor is whether the pastor is open to allowing a caring team to review his or her counseling. It may even be necessary, at times, to turn over to the caring team a counseling situation.

A congregation could decide that every couple who the pastor sees in premarital counseling or every couple who is to be married is expected to meet with the caring team. For a pastor to cooperate to this extent will indeed take an humble acceptance of the role as servant-leader.

12. A shepherding task must be accepted by every member.

This model assumes that members of the congregation will take the assignment of being one's "brother's keeper" literally (Genesis 4:9-11). They will accept that they are called to take on the task of being a spiritual friend to a faltering brother or sister and to gently guide the person in need to the caring team if that is appropriate.

One congregation officially designated a shepherd for every small group which was formed. The shepherds were instructed to keep a listening ear open at all times to persons in need. They were charged to inquire about the welfare of their assigned flock. They then contacted individuals in need from their assigned role of shepherd. If the need could not be met by the shepherds, they turned to the resources of the group. If any doubt arose, there was a team standing by to be called upon as a further resource.

13. The congregation and the caring team must have flexibility, imagination, and ingenuity.

To respond appropriately to the uniqueness of every needy situation, and the uniqueness of every individual or couple, the team needs to see its response as distinctively different at all times. If ever there is a place where the congregation must be creative and flexible, it is in the area of needy persons and problem marriages. This is true not only because of the complexity of every situation, but also because troubled persons expect a rigid doctrinal approach. At a time like this, the couple needs to know that they are cared for in a special way by a caring team delegated by the congregation, so that they can yield to the loving process in which they are asked to participate. For that to occur, there must be continued prayer that the team be used as delegates of God in whatever way is necessary to bring about healing.

At times it is best for the team to give oversight to a healing process while they themselves are only minimally involved. Every program, service, individual, or group within the congregation should be viewed as a possible resource. This helps the team not to lose sight of the fact that they are only a segment of the congregation, and never should do anything that is in conflict with the parent organization—the congregation. Even though a team of persons is responsible for a segment of the total congregational tasks, the other members of the church should be helped to see themselves as part of the spiritually and emotionally healing community.

14. There must be a congregation/team covenant.

In the final analysis, the effectiveness of the team and the congregation with hurting persons will depend on the willingness to be committed to a trusting relationship with others. This leads to a covenant of caring with others. The same covenant should exist between the caring team and the congregation.

Since many of the issues that must be faced are controversial, it is best that an atmosphere of the love of Christ pervade even when there are disagreements. The ultimate purpose is to bring about emotional and spiritual healing in the lives of hurting persons. That, after all, is the mission of the church.

Appendix A

Suggested Guidelines for the
Counseling Ministry Team

These guidelines were approved by the Council of Elders of a congregation with whom the authors worked.

1. Name of This Group

The name of this group shall be the Counseling Ministry Team. It seems appropriate to broaden the focus to include a wider range of needs which are brought to this group.

2. Overall Objective

The overall objective is to be a healing, guiding, and advising resource to all members of the congregation who are facing crises and require more help than can feasibly be given by the pastor, the Board of Elders, or individual church members. The main purpose will be to care for persons in crises, regardless of the nature of the need. The coordination of the team should be directed by the Minister of Pastoral Care, or other clinically trained person. Persons serving on the Counseling Ministry Team shall be appointed by the Council of Elders and the work of the team shall be reviewed annually by the Elders.

3. Specific Concerns

    a. Couples who are facing marital crises will be the concern of this team.

(1) A standing, public invitation will be presented to the congregation so that all members know that the team is available to help anyone in need.

(2) Contacts with the team may be made by couples-in-need or by other caring individuals who know of a hurting relationship.

(3) Team members may initiate a contact with couples who are experiencing a stressful relationship.

(4) The team will make referrals to resources outside the congregation for help when that seems most appropriate.

b. Couples asking to be married will be requested to meet with the Counseling Team for at least one session as part of the premarital counseling process.

c. Persons who are out of fellowship with another church member, or with another individual, may use the team to explore redemptive options. This is in line with the scriptural admonition in Matthew 18:15-20 on how to bring restoration between people who are at odds with each other. The team may initiate action towards reconciliation.

d. Those involved in grief ministry may use the team as a resource in ministering to the needs of persons who are facing or have experienced grief.

e. In divorce and remarriage situations, the team's primary task will be to guide individuals and couples to consider carefully the biblical position on these issues; to help individuals to be accountable for any sin that has been committed; and to seek forgiveness and a renewed relationship to Christ, to the church, and to each other.

4. Referral to the Team

a. Since the work of the team will be described to the congregation and reference made to it by the pastor, everyone in the congregation will be invited to make use of the team in times of crisis. *Absolute confidentiality* will be adhered to so that persons can trust the team to share their difficulties in strict confidence.

b. All separation, divorce, and remarriage situations will be dealt with by the team.

c. The pastor, already a member of the team, should feel free to discuss with the team any persons he sees in counseling, with the possibility that he receive help in guiding the counseling process.

d. All couples seeking marriage will be guided by the pastor to meet with the team as part of the process which the congregation has adopted in preparation for marriage.

e. Each team member will be free to invite members who appear to be in trouble to meet with her (him) and then guide them to a meeting with the caring team.

f. The Elders, Deacons, and Class Shepherds should be on the alert for persons who need more help than is appropriate for them to give and to shepherd a person or couple to the team.

g. Every church member could accept a shepherding role in that they should feel free to contact persons in need and care for them and then volunteer to go along to speak to a team member or to the entire group and meet with them for a session.

5. The Response of the Team

a. The overall purpose of this team is to structure a healing process for each situation it encounters. It will exercise the power of prayer and spiritual concern, as well as engage in a carefully guided healing process. It will encircle the person or couple with whatever resources are necessary to move toward greater spiritual, emotional, interpersonal, relational, and congregational wholeness.

b. The team will attempt to convey biblical principles and clarify the congregational position in every situation. Persons who are unable to submit to the church's position will be referred to the Council of Elders.

c. Existing small groups, or special small groups may be created and called upon to encircle a particular person or couple for extended support and fellowship. The team will give guidance to these groups as needed in specific crises situations.

d. When special problems arise, the team will call on persons in the congregation with needed gifts and/or training.

e. At times, persons will be referred to therapists or counselors outside the congregation for specialized help. The team may request to have these persons return at the end of the sessions to plan for their continuing welfare. A person's financial situation should not be a barrier to getting specialized help and Local Aid Funds can be used for such needs.

6. Membership of the Counseling Ministry Team

a. To assure greater confidentiality and to facilitate ease of meeting, the primary core group of the team would best be kept at 4-6 persons, represented in the following way:
—Pastor(s)
—Member(s) from the Council of Elders
—Clinically trained person(s)
—Representation from within the congregation which might include couples, divorced person(s), remarried person(s), single person(s).
Note: It is desirable that the work of the team be guided by a clinically trained person. While various representation is desirable, the most important criteria is that the person has the necessary gifts for this type of ministry.

b. No specific terms of service will be set. This type of ministry will call for a stable, long-term core of persons serving on the team. Persons serving on the team will be appointed by the Council of Elders and those appointments evaluated as part of their annual review of the work of the team.

c. The team shall be free to call on other persons within the congregation to assist the team in its ministry to persons such as in providing financial counseling, a ministry of prayer, a support group, etc.

Appendix B

A Sample Congregational
Statement Regarding Divorce and Remarriage

Realizing the scriptural teaching on the permanence of marriage, and yet recognizing the fact that in the fallen state of men and women some individuals do become involved in the serious problem of divorce and remarriage, we hereby resolve:

a. That marriage is intended by God to be a lifelong loving relationship between husband and wife. Matthew 19:4-6.

b. That the church should by teaching and other available means seek to enable marriages to reach their fullest potential and thus build strong family relationships.

c. That we recognize through human weakness and sin the "death" of marriage can occur. 1 Corinthians 7:15; Matthew 19:9.

d. That we accept our responsibility to deal redemptively and in a spirit of Christian love with those who have become involved in the problem of divorce and remarriage. John 8:3-11.

e. That we realize every Christian is a sinner forgiven by God, and thus avoid a judgmental attitude.

f. That it is the responsibility of the congregation to find solutions, under God's leading, for every situation that may arise.

It is, furthermore, resolved that each applicant for church membership who has been involved in divorce and remarriage shall be counseled by the pastors and elders, and upon evidence of repentance and the new-birth experienced in both word and action, shall be eligible for congregational approval.

Appendix C

A Sample Dedication and Wedding Service for Previously Married Persons

Invocation

Address to the People
Dear Friends. Your presence here today gives testimony to your belief in marriage and your well wishes for Harold and Ellen and the children.

The Scriptures say that marriage was instituted by God and is regulated by his commandment. (Read Ephesians 5:21-26.)

I. Dedication Service
Harold and Ellen, we have met together here today recognizing that an unexpected sequence of events in the lives of both of you has brought you, in the providence of God to a second marriage. Today we feel it appropriate to humbly acknowledge that the good and perfect will of God is that the first marriage, for all of us, shall endure through disappointment, heartaches, and tragedy. The breakup of marriages today is evidence that many times one or both partners are unwilling to remain faithful to the hard promises they made to each other.

Harold, we have been very close to the circumstances which brought your first marriage to despair and dissolution, and we do believe that neither of you wanted that to happen. We have been aware of the conscientious and heroic efforts which you have made to repair the broken marriage, and your willingness and eagerness to seek and abide by the counsel of Christian brothers and sisters. We believe that, had your previous partner been willing to do so, you were willing and eager to begin again to right whatever went wrong. But you have been divorced by your previous spouse, and in light of these facts, we meet here in the tender mercy and grace of God to unite you in a new marriage.

Do you, therefore, humbly acknowledge and receive forgiveness from God and these members of his family and your families, for the known and unknown aspects of the failure in your first marriage that may have been attributed to your lack of knowledge and your human limitations in living together in love with your first partner?

If so, Harold, please answer, "I do acknowledge my failure and humbly receive God's forgiveness."

Do you approach this new marriage determined to the best of your knowledge and ability to benefit from the experiences of the past by continuing to learn and grow in your capacity to live patiently and steadfastly in your relationships to each other, by the law of God's unconditional love, his unfailing mercy, and tender compassion for those who disappoint and fail you, even if one of those persons is your spouse? If so, answer, "I do, God helping me."

Ellen, for you especially, these vows you are about to take today involve five persons instead of one, for Harold's children are a significant part of himself and his life. Do you promise, therefore, to be a faithful Christian helper, friend, and adviser to these children, and to support and sustain them in their care and nurture and do your part in providing for them the atmosphere and opportunities which pertain to their spiritual growth and development? If so, answer, "I do, so help me God."

II. Wedding Service

Harold and Ellen, I do therefore present you to God and to these families and friends here assembled, for the purpose of uniting you together, contrite and cleansed, in holy matrimony.

Marriage is a gracious provision of God for meeting our human need to be accepted, loved, and sustained in an ever growing intimacy and responsibility.

It is ordained by God because he knows that we can neither survive nor mature if we abide alone and live for ourselves alone. He declares marriage to be a primary witness in our world of the never ending, sacrificial love of Christ Jesus for us, his bride. Jesus never leaves us nor forsakes us. He promises to be faithful in forgiving and cleansing us. He went so far as to die so that our lives could be better. He gives his strength and power to us every day, and he always prays for us. He makes available to us all his resources, and everything that belongs to Him will one day belong to us. That is the mystery and wonder of our relationship to Christ, that marriage is supposed to represent here on earth. It is a big order, but we can make it our goal and guiding light, and we can grow in our human capacity to behave in our marriages in all these needful and wonderful ways.

Marriage brings many deep joys and satisfactions which are not heavy with duty and responsibility, but one of the greatest satisfactions is in knowing that we have been loyal and faithful in difficulty and strong enough to endure in hard times. This is the challenge and reward which I offer to you today, as you now join hands and take these solemn vows.

Vows

I, Harold, take you, Ellen to be my wife, to have and to hold from this time forth, for better for worse, for richer for poorer, in health and in sickness, to love and to cherish till death us do part, according to God's holy ordinance, and with this ring I do pledge you my faith.

I, Ellen, take you, Harold, to be my husband, to have and to hold from this time forth, for better for worse, for richer for poorer, in health and in sickness, to love and to cherish till death us do part, according to God's holy ordinance, and with this ring I do pledge you my faith.

Pronouncement

By the authority committed to me as a minister of the gospel, I declare that Harold and Ellen are now husband and wife, according to the ordinance of God and the law of the state. In the name of the Father and of the Son and of the Holy Spirit. Amen.

What therefore God hath joined together, let not man put asunder.

Prayer
(For Harold and Ellen. . . . Then for the children, by name.)

Congratulations and Benediction

This service was prepared by Eber and Ruth Dourte, Dillsburg, Pa., a pastor and his wife (a marriage counselor), in consultation with the couple. We are grateful for their permission to include it in this book.

The Authors

A braham and Dorothy Schmitt have a deep commitment to the church and have been active members all of their adult lives. For several decades they have jointly conducted marriage enrichment retreats and other growth-related work-  shops in various church settings throughout North America. For ten years, Dorothy and Abe have been members of a team involved in counseling ministry at their home congregation.

The idea for this book evolved in the Mennonite congregation which Dorothy attended since infancy. (Her ancestors were members of this congregation since its beginning more than 225 years ago.) She was born in eastern Pennsylvania, attended public schools, and received a degree from Grand View Hospital School of Nursing. She also graduated from Goshen College, Goshen, Indiana, and joined the nursing faculty there in the early 1950s. Currently she is active on several congregational committees, including one on family life.

Abe's origins were an Old Colony Mennonite village in Saskatchewan. In a cluster of twenty villages, people cared for each other's needs. Everything that happened to a person or a family deeply affected members of the community.

Abe left to attend Rosthern Junior College and Canadian Mennonite Bible College, and then crossed over to the United States to attend Goshen College and Goshen College Biblical Seminary. Following their marriage, Abe became a member of Dorothy's home congregation.

Education again took precedence as Abe received his master's and doctor's degrees from the University of Pennsylvania. This led to an interdisciplinary professorship in the Department of Psychiatry, the School of Social Work, and the Marriage Council. He also held clinic positions at a variety of psychiatric facilities.

Currently Abe has a private practice in individual and marital therapy in Souderton, Pennsylvania.